FUTURESTO

FUTURESTO

Musings on Shape of Things to Come

There is enough for everyone

*"Authors unknown hereof
Penned by an unpaid scribe
Revealing known secrets
In long spells of fruitful toil
Bearing nature's mandate:
Peace in air, space 'n land
To abide by freedoms four."*

Puran C. Gururani

Vol. I

PARTRIDGE
A Penguin Random House Company

ISBN: Softcover   978-1-4828-1305-0
                Ebook   978-1-4828-1306-7

To order additional copies of this book, contact
Partridge India
000 800 10062 62
www.partridgepublishing.com/india
orders.india@partridgepublishing.com

CONTENTS

Signpost 3: Shape of Things

Chapter 3:

Signpost 4: Wanderlust of Thought

Chapter 4:

Signpost 5: Return to your Roots

Signpost 6: Encounter with God

Signpost 7: Bulls & Bears

Chapter 7:

Signpost 8: Miscellaneous

Chapter 8:

*"Proceeds from this publication
Will go for human causes
In whatever little way they can—
Keep track for possible lapses"*

Introduction

A manifesto is the documented public pronouncement of a Political Party's action-plans for the betterment of the circumstances of the people of its country. Likewise, *'FUTURESTO'* is the writer's attempt, taking inspiration from the futuristic ideas of the wise men and women of history, to highlight the need for structural changes in the existing doddering old institutions concerned with the management of the temporal affairs of the people. Because, over the years, they have become loaded with the tar of venality, self-seeking, mammon worship and what not.

The turbulence, bloody conflicts, widespread dissatisfaction the world over with vague moralization and sabotage of egalitarian values are too ominous signs to ignore. Leisurely pursuit of economics of profit, extravagant jamborees vulgarizing cultural tastes, the practice of adversarial politics of spoils and the sordid amalgam of the secular with the ecclesiastical cannot continue for long. The plaintive notes of humanity are inked in the *'FUTURESTO'* to generate interest and debate on the urgency of the changes needed. And at the same time explore the protean capacity of democracy to throw up new guidelines for management of the temporal affairs of humankind, through concerted efforts at the national and international levels, so that we all are able to live and prosper together, balancing human aspirations with the limitations of nature.

Prof. Puran C. Gururani

Acknowledgement

As it is customary to do so, the curator of the ideas contained in this volume is obliged to all those writers and thinkers of the past and there is no end to thank them. A word or two are due to the one person who has painstakingly over the last few years has worked hard along with the Curator to see that this volume comes into life and in public domain. The Curator cannot fully thank and express his gratitude to his granddaughter, Damini Tewari, a PhD student at King's College London but for whom this collection of poems would not have seen the light of the day.

A word may also be written to thank and express my gratitude to the hard working housewife who let me get engaged in this type of work and to neglect all my household responsibilities. That person is no other than my caring and loving wife.

Chapter 1

There Is Enough For Everyone

Bones Don't Cry

Mother where's all the flesh from me gone
You said was part of mine when I was born
It was soft silky sacramental and so lovely
Gave me life and vigor and made me cry
Mother you didn't talk of bones then, why

Mom these bones don't hurt don't demand
Its the poky pit with some flesh still around
Called tummy that pains and makes me cry
Renders me miserable crazy and mindless
Crave for food that is not ample or is mine

Mother take away that little remnant flesh
From shriveled belly still sticking around
Fill it with more bones there that abound
I will crave not for food or for sacred life
Nor for a patch of land as mine to survive

Nor for them fussy few to come in between
Give me those rotten smelly morsel or two
Put my dry frame on canvas and click away
Depart in tearing haste saying god bless you
Mother you shedding tears shamelessly why

My tears are dry flesh gone bones don't cry
Mother you said militiamen maim and hurt
For a cut of land arid faith heavenward bound
As if there is not enough of an abiding space
For all those born in this placid mother earth

God's home called heaven by genteel imagery
Will not let in even the clerics among them
For their failure to see between sin and piety
Who kill in God's name and deign to sell faith
Will die a wretched death at their own hands

Even copious hell has no place for such of them
Who have nothing except gooey fungous faith
Plied irreverently on slushy putrid brand loyalty
Holding tattered piece of parchment as authority
Its no faith that allows killing staking wantonly

Mother you would be God's darling to shred faith
Piece by piece and offer it to ravenous wolves
To secure the life of man God's only testimony
Let not our plentiful earth be charred by acrimony
Do restore sanity secure sanctity of human entity

Razzle Dazzle Inequity

It's billed the poor have to live
For the uppity rich to survive
Live and die in stink and filth
For elite 'n parasites to sanitize

Letting go their life and liberty
For them few to hypothesize
Amass their riches on slippery
Counter of rigged opportunity

Malice 'n hatred piled on them
Whom living is lawfully denied
Who burn dung cakes to bake
Their meagre musty hard bread

Drink filth rich municipal water
Breathe immensely polluted air
Eat adulterated infected grain
Create harbour for bacteria wide

Manoeuvre to live sans ceremonies
Under burden of democratic strains
For few elites to reason and plead
And call it debit of their past deeds

Ghosts of the poor whine pitifully:
"You'll have to catch up quickly
To even the score roll up destiny
Clear agonizing mist of villainy"

Elites burn others souls to balm theirs
Perfume sagging skins to suppress
Irrepressible heavy funerary stink
Of acquisition from plundering

The old wobbly ship of humanity
With razzle dazzle heap of inequity
Tilts sideways creates little upset
Among poor dumb human ballast

But the uppity meddlesome men
Are sucked in by dark churn of ocean
Their creeds cults 'n philosophies
Heartless civilizations unavailing

Though it has not been said so wisely
That heaven shall belong to the poor
But the poor indeed will redeem earth
Make it a safe heaven of their own

God Suffers when Poor are in Agony

I saw this mussy man laugh boisterously
Was it the nature's way of celebrating life
Dark with hunger, starvation skinned him
Stinking, had no gutter water to wash even

Heart beating strong but body had no flesh
Eyes straddling horizon, gruel was not near
Saw birds chasing in blue sky gallantly
Ecstasy ended as eagle condensed length

Swooped on the one boisterous and flirty
Others thanked heavens for the life spared
This mussy man is not affected by avarice
Contempt nor even curse curls his dry lips

Scorn and belly fire he fights intensely
Burns his soul imploring high heavens
To pounce upon ninny life left forlorn
He calls earthy denial a divine design

His mother had told him uncomplainingly
Those who make others suffer go to hell
Heaven's meant for them who suffer meekly
God too suffers when the poor are in agony

Different Kind of El Dorado

Wavering mind lecherous legends stony heart
Are the sole wealth of the nerdy man of pride
Who conceals in his bosom hatred of himself
He lives in certitude, none except him knows
That there's a prison where he alone resides
Along with crime, people see as an opportunity,
Knows neither reason nor hope can redeem him

He knows full well hope's abode is despair
Ever widening is thinness of vagrant thought
False faith beleaguered beliefs taboos totems
Cannot redeem and make him human again
Unless all that society stands for takes pride in
Sheltered in the impregnable past, is annulled
To recover oyster from ocean of falsehood

Else utter ruin pain beyond tolerance limits
Will face human society huddled incarcerated
In rhetoric of history, its awful weird hatred
Civilization's boisterous jamboree unavailing
We know not there are realms of conscience
Ensconced in the heart and in resplendent mind
More ennobling than all promises of heaven

To be able to commiserate and live with grace
Standing at cross-roads of misbelief confused
Man has to take the fresh and unbeaten track
Leading to a very different kind of El Dorado
Where gold is not priced nor stored or fancied
Only trust and honour are of any consequence
Where goods are not marketed nor exchanged

But are made available on the human mandate
Which our nations as yet are unable to manage
Pearl S. Buck said: "Food for all is a necessity
Food shouldn't be a merchandise to be bought
And sold as jewels by those who have money
Like water and air it should be available free"
To regain the heaven of freedom lost in greed

Why you should listen to sages old and gone
Coz they delved deep to cull natures secrets
For us all to celebrate life avoid pitfalls
Nature spreads its wealth for all to share
A bread shared makes two happy none scared
So do be good as much as you can, possibly may
"As you can't enter the same river twice"

In Compassion Alone Man will Endure

What shall you do with such a vision
Which is barnacled makes you foggy
Puts clammy hands on your forehead
Cajoling to condone atrocities on men

Committed by misanthropes 'n maniacs
To descerate civilizations and religions
Posing as faith healers peace purveyors
With apothecary's bag spreading myths

Robbing many of conscience in bargain
By lousy make-believe 'n tutored counsels
Misshape their values by vibrancy of vices
Liquidating all reason of its authenticity

Man has not been blessed nor ever bonded
But always badgered besieged bludgeoned
Into pulp by verbose conscience tricksters
Putting his native genius in faith-shackles

All suffering is multiple, sighs are private
The child in us has become an irascible ape
Never a pious belief gentle faith dewy love
Flowers in itchy thickets of brazen thought

Has ever a tear rolled down the closed eyes
From a heart untouched by intense remorse
Without tears sorrows forever turn abrasive
Burning pain isn't relieved by frozen relief

Above our garnished knowledge there exits
A vast region of substance vitality and bliss
It enkindles and drives men do heroic deeds
Calls them to envision an ascendant humanity

Faith and compassion lie not in gilded relics
But in uncluttered and plain commandments
In sharing and caring, pruning venal desires
Alone humans will survive fate of dinosaurs

Revenue of Heart

O commissar don't change all that is around you
Change is not enduring nor always commendable
Vestiges of old memories well nigh remain alive
To triumph over the hostile doctrinaire change

O priest do not infect the sacred springs of life
By deadly dope of unreason 'n sermonized malice
Hope and love alone endure for ever, not jealousy
Don't ever taint them by your piquant obduracy

Tender love is the ever solvent revenue of heart
Faith-mongers can't hope to reach it nor scourge it
Or mutilate it thru deceitful meaningless verbosity
Better to go slow on dogma, half-brother of heresy

Future is not far distant but very much near at hand
But out of sync with flexi time and salacious trends
You can't think of putting past present and future
In separate compartments of your accursed choice

Its time you change the portfolio of hate and malice
Beacon of hope will guide humanity to chosen shores
Currency of love will sure bank in peace and amity
In such a world there'll be no place for venal legacy

Coz human mind is not subject to laws of entropy
Nor even ephemeris or any kind of prognosis reveal
Extent of immesurable font of convertible energy
Rooted in love as can end all divides of destiny

Don't Know Why I Cried

I don't know why I cried
But it was good that I did
Rolling tears washed away
All the dirt from my mind

I cry seeing a skinny child
Eating scanty grub in smiles
I cry seeing a lean lanky one
Walking forlorn not fearful

Unwary of hunger torn soles
The end of dreary road in mind
To home nowhere near at hand
Just to be in his mother's arms

Sobs screams of impaled souls
Flail me I cry for humankind
I cry as warring couples part
I cry as they forgive 'n forget

I cry for dawn of plentiful life
With love peace 'n honey bee
To lessen the chores of journey
To the promised land of equity

Spa of Enlightenment

I value the little things in life hurt and hapless
A child in the slums the beggar by the roadside
Or a family shattered through a misguided man
Left with nothing but just a faint forlorn heart
They all are too frail to take care of themselves
Mind sans ripples not even eyes that can see far
Needing attention endearing touch kind words

For them higher arts literatures soulful sermons
Swanky fetes of life, meaningless solicitations
Have no attraction, these are vapid fulminations
Often lacking coherence considered misbegotten
To them misery shared small discomfort undertaken
Are pleasures incomparably more blissful humbling
Spa of enlightenment soothing liberating the mind

My gods are those who have hunger in their tummies
Hopes in their hearts and benediction in dusky eyes
Minds are free from the fever of smouldering hate
Full of love from nameless births unmourned deaths
They don't fight over a morsel of smelly rotten food
Vitamins and calories free and coarse as their bodies
Live under thatched roofs by the trees bereft of leaves

Cluster together send their prayers to high heavens
For peace on sacred earth comfort for fellow beings
Friends foes, life on land oceans and for vegetation
There are no Gods as noble in the cosmos as them
They are the salt of Earth soul of our civilization
May the number of such Gods multiply day 'n night
To save humankind from horrors of vengeful rites

Yearn To Write That Line

I yearn to write that fulsome line:
As will tell the story of whole life
Live for days and not wrinkles see

Love to see how long hate can last
And recapture redolent memories
To guess how far indeed future be

Above all I fondly wish to reconcile
The irreconcilables just to find out
How much the other man was right

I yearn to write that fulsome line:
As will tell story of lonesome youth
Ravished by wintry famine of love

In search of the heady nectar of life
With eyes not so posited on forehead
But embedded in heart's ample space

Peering into serene eternity where
Like bird-song in spring ever echoes
Tingling hope cascading into ecstasy

I yearn to write that fulsome line:
As will tell the story of the child
At mother's breast who she caresses

"Be a good man with motherly heart
Father's bold endearing countenance
Like trusty lamppost on a snowy night

As you blossom kindred soul, dear me
Be a guiding spirit to whoever in need be
World is full of treasures for everybody

Reach them with a feather touch of mercy
To those whom cruel fate has ill conspired
Make love not leered by pleasures messy"

Dawn from Pregnant Night

My India shall you wake up anon
Siren sirens bell bells drum drums
Alarum alarums blast blasts burns
Quake quakes upheaval upheavals
Holocaust 'n kills, Destiny is that us

Oh no India shall wake up, yes anon!
But no point to wake up in a world
Exhausted within 'n naked outside
Gives neither a home nor a hearth
Or fulsomeness of beguiling hopes

Only a mute awesome loneliness
Meshed up in lust lucre nit-wit love
In a catastrophic rush to nowhere
Is that awakening, let India lie low
In poverty and ruthless exploitation

Heartless hunger not of her making
Forsooth, retaining her true identity
Indian to its roots but a little dimsy
Others' world is worse woebegone
Wherefrom dear hope escaped slyly

It's a civilization on wheels of woes
Cursed body wanton splitting of heart
Pulled and pushed by contrary visions
Faith and culture split by perversion
Our pain is small theirs a feral farce

Let India lie low in its wretchedness
Ensconced in her heart is ever present
The hope of a dawn from pregnant night
India shall soon wake up unrepentant
As light spreads and animalism exits

The torch lighted in this land illumines
Homes of peoples in blessed earth
Who live happily in harmony amity
Glows still in hearts full of empathy
Will beat darkness in minds vacillating

Womb

Nature was so kind to have created a womb
In the body of a fine person who won't shirk
To carry the mantra of life from seed to seed
So that the affidavit of culture is not reneged

It is an art box similar in shape 'n substance
Supple and alike in colour flesh and size
Harbours many legends of love 'n sacrifice
Carries the hope of a better human species

Womb abjures myths of race place creed
Shelters foetus from the elemental vagaries
Nature then sets in to claim its own copyright
Gives it community a place to call its own

It matures 'n develops a sense of belonging
Becomes heir to songs sagas of his forbears
Womb took million years to perfect its code
The world of humans will sure follow suit

Nature's bounties are not same everywhere
Sun and the moon illumine not every place
Don't lose hope, the womb took nine months
To give one with a centurion promise of life

Humans too will develop a similar ambiance
In due time to transcend nature's limitations
If they follow their hearts keep minds in order
And never ever sponge on their neighbours

Counterfeit

I seem to have seen you somewhere:
May be on a dung heap of deception
On road to forgery a winsome game
May be at a jagged counter of shame
Or else, you sure have mistaken me

Not for the nonce I was respectable
Charity I know not nor shown to me
Nobility sure I do have save by birth
Humanity though not misplaced in me

Behind the heavy veil of culture
I have known the dubious 'n dregs
Care I least for men with fake piety
Vicious but ever in search of an alibi

Prithee cease to bother in short life
About fate or enquire into destiny
For it all will spin to a stop one day
Baring valid truth from deep ocean
Of teeming doubts for mortals to swig

All that glitters is not gold nor good
To live in dank hovels is no shame
But to earn your daily keep by fraud is
To labour love 'n shower little mercies
Is within our wits all else is counterfeit

Lofty Principle of Survival

Rains came darkness descended lightning struck
I huddled with my kinsfolk under the yonder tree
Like I had done before many times out of number

Rains stopped darkness dispelled and the sun rose
Fresh winds cruised, and the birds chirped merrily
The river passed by in soft singing ripples quietly

I thanked gods and begged for their ample grace
Thanked darkness lightning thunder and rains
Which had taken kindly to me and to my tribe

Because in the yester-year they had swept away
Those spiteful villains who ventured in the rains
To drive away my poor neighbour's only cow

I thank the gentle rains for abundance they bring
Droughts taught me they have some other regions
To shed their weight and shower their blessings

Made us learn to build granaries and to store
Just in case, to survive but not in selfishness
Save 'n share it with whosoever be in distress

Frigid Tradition

Mildewed eyes burning mind and a crafty will
How long will man traverse the hazy path
Strewn with litter of ages much mistrodden
Forking into hundred alleyways blind spots

Born in a world chequered by cults 'n creeds
Forums institutions cast in decaying plaster
On old moulds same in depths and contours
Man has done little so frigid are the traditions

But the child of God must bewitch the Satan
Turn down that's stood for ages dark 'n grey
Thump the old clay with vigour 'n build anew
Over deep laid foundations, enduring forms

As have sheen vibrant twists 'n sweep of old
Blended with symphonious notes of modernity
The discerning prefer new wardrobe of thought
With neat upper cut and smooth linear designs

Against the filigreed trappings of yesteryears
Unlacerated by confusion of itsy bitsy fashions
Comfortable compendious dapper long lasting
Wholesome but not smocked by uppity bracings

What after all are traditions if not ideas 'n codes
Invalidated by usage atrophied by flux of time
So let not traditions ever seize the body in maze
And wayward thoughts add to shoddy baggage
Styles of life that frisky trends do not deflect
Should be the preferred bet of man of intellect

Chapter 2

Ship of Democracy

Ship of Democracy

Democracy is a safe cruise and a fine voyage
Across the balmy blue oceans in fair weather
Over the rippling rolling frothy white waves
Hauled by the majority and minority strokes

Come high seas or the crushing choppy waters
Ship of democracy packed with hope warriors
Is astir with diminutive hulky busy buddies
Braving minority strokes once majority thence

Rolling democracy's ship violently sideways
Crew clueless master sightless ship in shoals
Risking lives of voyagers with hope baggage
In the rising tumult a listless voyager hails:

"Put away gusty majority 'n minority strokes
Jettison the garbage of history shun razzmatazz
Remember insular minority is a well fed shrew
Majority, a blind muffing mean fellow brute

Huddle in center away from battered boards
Lift unthinking rudder, push shove patiently
Don't muddy the waters striking in a frenzy
Democracy will ferry suspecting humanity

Over uncharted oceans billowing high seas
Banking by virgin shores spread peace 'n amity
Build new institutions housing freedoms four
For mankind to live free from fear 'n scourge"

Democracy needs be given a fresh nectar bath
Clean it, smutted it is with the mud of stupidity
Journey is long times ominous but its old sails
Will take us to our cherished land without fail

Corridors of power darkened by deceit savagery
By those full of ego greed and feverish frenzy
History shows only hope is clean lean democracy
Peace by peace is its unending quiet advocacy:

"You shall not assemble fools knaves 'n bookies
To elect vandals loaded with the tar of venality
It's time to call gentlemen to select gentlemen
To man ship of democracy to run affairs of men
It is an insignia of humankind's sumumbonam"

God is a democrat, rears up what He creates
Has the same fare for all who live by His grace
Expects us to do the same in our assigned roles
Let not politicians ruin it by their venal embrace

I Had a Dream

I had a dream a dream in sound sleep
It's awfully sharp like sunlight beam
I huddled in a corner guess it was dark
Light disturbs me fear of being found
By preachy preceptors in aerial mounts

Only thing common among us I found
Two peering eyes long hands bow-legged
Eerie plaintive music reminiscing elegies
Rest was savage, skin under bristling hair
Frightening warlike cries extolling gods

Their wild stomping feet staccato strains
Made me run away from horrid dream
To my conscience spluttering to be free
Now I fear being reminded of preceptors
Even if world of wealth 'n wine is on offer.

Next, saw Democracy Boat ferry humans
Dark brown red and some big and small
Across the gusty river to shores not near
Humming lilting tunes of hope and peace
A fidgety few raving at the slow speed

Asked others to jump swim in full steam
Few swam gustily some distance dismayed
The leader lost breath rest in pandemonium
Few more jumped unhappy with their stay
Undeterred by ruinous vain mad venture

More intrepid ones challenged status quo
Many more impatient ones met the same fate
Rest of quite pilgrims full of prayers 'n hope
Were soon anchored safe holding their fort
As Democracy Boat quietly made to the shore

Follow Me

I will fain pursue that peerless unity
Tryst her with my heart and serenade
Encompassing simple verities of life
I'll muster the thought that transcends
The evanescent glimmer of frothy power
Speak of joy ensconced in human hearts

I will recreate the frisky fibers of peace
Colour them with the mirth of living
Small mercies all I need to be blessed
My abode is an adorned crest of quest
Of light hope abiding peace 'n amity
Negotiating rapids of contending bodies

Pray, join me in my tryst, it's the only
Unerring beacon of hope 'n fair play
To build viable bridges to human peace
Wisdom 'n power gently inhere in me
Dare say, I can serve the frail humanity
With the wholeness of my ample being

Still be full 'n faithful as galley sails
I'm no riddle my name is Nations Unies
It is all peoples' love filled jamboree
Help me to deal with faceless anomie

Since wars begin in the minds of men
Defences of peace do be built therein
Render to men what history decreed
Begin a new calendar of peace amity

Let not world be pushed by feuding bodies
Mean men persuing ruinous designs
Risking precious wisdom 'n copious gains
Earned in years in civilizational pains

World Citizen

Nations 've usurped peoples' quiet blessed world
Politicians have usurped fickle nations in turn
Incestuous power lust has usurped the politics
There is no scope or place left for the rest of us

Lords leaders lumpen leeches dumb followers
Fathers mothers friends foes sailors 'n soldiers
Are manipulated to serve nations put in blinkers
Made to do things terribly inhuman and heartless

Enthused to commit dire deeds in collaboration
Raised to flashpoints of division and destruction
But for a wise few, rest fired by false inspiration
Pushed by promise of plentiful bonanza in return

Nations are managed mangled to benefit a few
Pamphleteers preceptors politicians fagin fools
Rest, meek and needy, left at the mercy of djinn
Dumb ballast in the sinking ship of civilization

Chickened and tongues held in leash mute many
Are paraded echoing war cries, "*death to enemy*"
Then tamely returned to their toiling pursuits
For safety and prosperity of nation's parasites

Seizures decrees and self made code of conduct
Make nations fight if their self interest is defied
Declaring others hate mongers dreaded beasts
In marathon run of rack 'n ruin, the poor bleed
Nations gather lustfully to redefine boundaries
With vows, charter of rights, fetish of apology
To continue the treacherous pursuits as before
In celebration of vengeful, fractured victories

Winners then gather to foster an illegal body
With flesh, spirit of their vaunted hypocrisies
Burdening world's poor with flabby structures
Splitting others' lives only to safeguard theirs

Nature sets limits, nations being no exceptions
It will squelch the gory march of civilization
With their corrugated laws scripted to deprive
Creators of wealth, who are driven to oblivion

World won't last criss-crossed by boundaries
Its peoples' right to move without restrictions
Settle anywhere create wealth by honest means
Bank for human affluence sans personal balance

Time to abandon fetishes forge new designs
Broaden spheres of human concern end strifes
Free from yoke of inheritance, for peace 'n order
Well worth world citizen to breathe freedoms four

Mighty Circus : Civil Secretariat

Dowdy chairs have eloped with dirty tables
Racks of files are raving in dimlit corridors
Corridors are running too but the old matador
The stately peon duly sits on fractured stool

What dust 'n cluster within mildewed almirahs
Where sun enters not nor air stays for vacuum
Decisions forsooth languish in due precedence
Within plated parchments of Whitehall brand
Insulated from the corrosion of time by red tape

Reformers in efficiency have braved high seas
On perforated board lousy sail and poky keel
Yahoo! fishermen on shores jeered ex-protocol
May be, sighting pen voyagers on a tin sieve

Reformers have vowed as before if venture fails
To blame it on wizened clerks lugubrious scribes
What baleful elements these to fight on high seas
When ammunition is short and vision foggy

A blighty circus on earth is Civil Secretariat
Giants waggling aimlessly in impromptu haste
Manikins haul the burden of a cracking frame
Here Fabius' art is practiced to neat perfection

For long I was commuting in its dimlit corridors
Carting bureaucracy's burden sagely as I could
They were days of little reward much hassled life
Regret was the only way of cajoling tired minds

Its now a den of starched unconscionable people
Goaded by bullish ego merit purloined from others
Failures blamed on norms beyond human control
Success pinned on chests swollen with insolence

Johnnies come lately of dubious provenance ask
To applaud the good tidings not of their making
Sham success pinned slyly on pallid performance
Drumming the ascent of Caesar of grey eminence

Stinking wealth concealed under messy frame
Who thieves when thieves are the prized trophy
In its labyrinths only shadows haggle aimlessly
What worth is left to call it the Civil Secretariat

Leaders' Chutzpah

Leader lost to himself in the crowd lonely
In vain he cajoles inveigles and harangues
Them to listen to his electric prescriptions
Yells in passionate frenzy but none listens

Winds are roaring gales 'n storms are astir
Skies hurtling down piercing bright beams
On crowd which in despair is turning away
Leader will never know what crowd needs

He raves 'n rants with a lump in his throat
Shorn of hope tries to whip up their sprits
Vows vents unmindful of emptying fields
In desperation promises what he can't yield

He is a creature of juncture but never upset
Darned 'n restored tries to reinvent himself
Thus rejuvenated he returns to the hustings
A much better grain from his earlier strain

Sugary words can't clear dense melancholy
Visions of future pushed by hope of arrival
Are just not enough to bring cheers to any
Promises never cure nor relief parry agony

Values are reared to be crushed, men picked
From history's depth as heirs to repression
To atone for sins of forbears not of their own
Civilization an old farce everywhere the same

Deadly at the bottom meddlesome at the top
Infidels rogues vandals emerge from within
Leaders' vows sag, bony prophets' quietened
Echoes resound in the misty corridors of time

Signifying dreaded eerie hollowness of it all
If pirated beefy sermons 'n loud ringing calls
Could blend loose metaphors of our destiny
Saints 'n sinners won't be supping in company

Music Stool

Sign in and sign off fast no time to wait
Its not a party O! fool no hope for broth
Its govt on music stools all assembled
In the backyard one for him one for boss

Others are for those who have no briefs
Who not worth their quality or integrity
But just assembled so that the deputies
Dare not topple him and spoil the party

Who runs the grand party 'n pays for it
No one knows, but there are dark faces
Who need no cover, all are accomplices
The party over the dark faces rake it all

All heist sliced from the nation's gross
Crumbs thrown to the people in stalls
Busy holding the fort at safe distance
With no choice got to listen to the boss

This whirligig isn't likely to end soon
Its the stool perfected by that wise man
To pass it on from gene to generations
Dumb followers say hurrah to his vision

Savages lived in caves had fellow feeling
City dwellers suffer from lack of trust
Incurrred through pride, widening anomie
Close the chasm or be ready for apoclypse

Macho Politicians

Whenever two politicians meet
One thing they find in common
Its their dislike for each other
Both know friendship a disaster

        But enmity a collapse per se
        Better, friendship in short run
        Against despair in the long one
        Know they've two faces each

One for self other for that bloke
Both at ease as line is crossed
No going back fate is common
Fall humiliating 'n unacceptable

        Life's no full stops only comas
        Trust and honesty are for a toss
        It helps to pretend bonhomie
        One without other is catastrophe

Eminence Grise

Politicians of any lens have great eminence
Learned men can't be compared with any of them
Their list of passions privileges has no end
Have a pedigree inheritance name 'n fame

Their big hearts throb with tainted blood
Winning or losing they remain the same
Have a world brotherhood to sustain them
Survive on false claims thrive on blame game

Don't trust any promises they really make
Falsehood their faith religion fishy bait
Disgusted, God threw them from His Heaven
Have made our good earth a sickening den

There is no escape from their dragon grip
Unless we burn the place called assembly
Along with ballot papers election tally
Together with their agents lumpen buddies

Savages monarchs dictators had their times
Politicians have ruled the roosts for too long
Its now time to kick them all bag 'n baggage
And call gentlemen to serve the gentlemen

Those who have excelled in their professions
To bring accumulated wisdom, proven gains
To bear on people's problems at no expense
World rescued from the dreaded grey eminence

Spoils of Politics

High and low wise or otherwise rich or the poor
All love politics, it ups their spirits lifts minds
Its half brother **business** is ready there at the corner

To gather ill-gotten gains made in polished scams
Nobody ever loses when business 'n politics thrive
Everybody moves up, assets as well as govt's pride

Rising standards errant pleasures vain comforts
Feverish crush of business, glare of politics of profits
Stupefies the clueless masses with haze of opulence

Hapless peoples all over the world are craven scared
Fear to breathe even lest fabled house of cards
Resplendent gilded inside out is blown to winds

Its flamboyant incumbents are rendered homeless
Its open secret that those in business of profits
Lawfully pass on loses they make to the god-forsaken.

Invoke providence to change murky business deeds
To resurrect innocence buried under debris of greed
Wait for its abolition if not today sure in near future

Chapter 3

Shape of Things to come

River of Rage

I am a soldier lying lugubriously with smitten face
On the sullied banks of the swollen River of Rage
Overflowed all over, clouds bemoaning hoards of them
Vultures watching waiting for tumult to settle down
To swoop on me tear apart raiment of vanished glory
Betokening splendour of the star studded regalia once

Eat through the mutilated visage into my darned heart
Turned black with malice and hatred born elsewhere
Lodged in me stealthily to fight out the vicious boor
The damned soldier on the other bank of River of Rage
To meet same fate surely as that of mine unrequited
Cruelly trampled deep under the vulgar pussy disdain
By conscienceless nasty brutes whose vision is leprous
Mired by sickening fantasy of the inflamed mind

Bursting fury of savages who ravaged civilizations
First muzzled the bodies of soldiers in utter disdain
Unlamented unrecalled, who die for others' causes
Then gored those of farmers tending fields not theirs
Workers sweating in funerary factories not of choice
Frail cheerless commoners peddling others' wares
Flurried intellectuals fence sitters and craven clerics
All were hauled over white heat of sweeping avarice
In pursuit of fanaticism and bloodshed of worst kind
Morbid phantasmagoria of the darkened dense minds
In the end the dead as always conquer faceless death

It is the grisly fare doled out by that boorish history
Slithering through blood rapine putrid heap of carcass
To those lying on both the banks of the River of Rage
Hither once thither thence in nostalgic reminiscence
Marking up scores of history's guiles 'n despoliation

Erelong the victorious and vanquished gather around
To gobble wealth garnered in deep chests of nations
Handiwork of faceless millions in long spells of toil
Treasures change hands, authority 'n power redefined
Positions exchanged, tyrants dethroned and throned

Everything thereafter is comely 'n placid as ever before
Not for those lying on either bank of the River of Rage
In heaps with dismembered bodies, charred aspirations
Licking pussy wounds incurred in pitiless vain sacrifice
By unsuspecting naive humanity, bargained to prop up
Gory pleasures of hawkish peers of rakish civilization
Waiting to be swooped in turn by swollen River of Rage
As it busts banks of hate 'n garish vulgarity unrepentant
Turning into slush the pride of nations their civilizations

Is there any hope from this whirligig of a suppurating cuss
Of course, if soldiers on either bank of the River of Rage
Who have seen enough of blood and gore age after age
Cadaverous faces stony eyes and minds borne on despair
Refuse bloodletting for other's sake in wars not their own

Give up arms renounce those who seek domain of history
A darkened den where even the dead nor living sojourn
Yes, if our folks never forge bonds with tyrants 'n lunatics
Who blinded by paranoia bigotry, glorify hatred 'n villainy
Mutilate millions who have same urge for amity and unity

Mother earth bares her treasures for one and all aplenty
Groomed this chic planet caringly as her only sojourn
Mess not in space care for this sole solitaire in cosmos
For no two stars in the teeming universes are the same
She is kind, not our kindred, may pardon but not forget
Angered, will destroy ugly structures that encumber her
To save herself, may spawn a new breed of supermen
Like of whom you daren't face in your wildest dreams
Time, humans to reverse the gear listen to voice within

Is it difficult to figure out why all kinds of idiologies
Are in the front row and goodmen are on the run
God not even in the last row, is doomsday near at hand
Yes, advent of new civilization is on the beams awaiting
Epiphany of pious aims 'n resolutions to burst upon us
To redeem our conscience choked by vain pursuits
And usher in a new era free from all kinds of delusions

World Criss-Crossed by Hate

In my vision there's the vision of seven billion people
Mirrored on the face of this blessed plentiful Earth
And something also of those who walked past history
In long coat-tails, traders tormenters soldiers 'n serfs
Parasites, revellers, hooky preachers 'n the credulous
Who all have walked to dusty end despite their intent
Leaving sickening tales for their progeny to contend

On my face there are signatures of seven billion people
Fascinated with themselves, turn of a superfluous nose
Curls in the hair, curvatures of ears and cusped lips
Eyes grey turquoise large and cagy as well as squint
Irises show many rainbow stripes of celestial rings
Many are the races their profiles all are coded in me
Many colours carelessly spread black red 'n swarthy

I have been moving on the bosom of this placid Earth
For countless centuries through vicissitude 'n violence
Bending on history why it calls darkened spots as glory
Some red 'n yellow black 'n white rest grey as gravel
Like the vacuous puckered faces of history's urchins
Seated in a dark corner of cobbled streets to nowhere

A faulty fuse in our mind trips light into utter darkness
Riches rags pride 'n piety mothered in the same womb
Yet alike in many ways and different in some others
Some are happy others are unhappy for reasons unclear
Warped by insularity in a world criss-crossed by hate
With very little of worth left to promote take pride in

Humans settle for what is to your mutual satisfaction
Reaching out to make the pool of values get still richer
It's not power of plenty but the desire to live together
That's the code for opening the chests of high treasure
Time to remove the mask of febrile fuss of class vanity
Kills conscience blurs vision is worse than ***rigor mortis***

World: A Can of Worms

A master artist is perched atop steep hill
Holding tight the canvas of aches and pain
Paints it with a luminous touch of empathy
His motto is do good as much as you can
Though the world is a nasty can of worms

Paints rainbows atop hills reaching heavens
Crystal river rippling by well watered lands
Little birdie calmly wooing pompous dawn
He splashes bright colours of joy all around
To raise the spirits of men and enrich minds
Summons their courage, the content of life
Stirs hope pulsating in their tender hearts
Insulates their minds from unclear preachers
Awakens conscience to live as nature willed
In collateral peace with all the living entities

An artist alone can open the can of worms
For all to see venal heritage of nerdy men
His brush is versatile God looks askance
Nothing will come out of the vain pursuits
Higgledy piggledy on bill board of history

A master artist needs, to pursue his mission,
A fertile soil full of the legends of antiquity
With ugly maggots running at cross purposes
Brooding knaves with their insular visions
A world full of slayers of virtues and values

Canvas stretched for master strokes of beauty
Convergence of humans full of sensitivity
Aspiring to trump evils to nurse humanity
To survive the bombast of bloated snobbery
The fiddle faddle of isms their acidic bigotry

Exuberant humans will indeed come of age
Acquiring vibrant wings to explore afresh
And discover secrets of the convoluted space
To perpetuate the biogenetic content of Earth
And conserve the little left to save their race

Ragamuffin to Newman

Dear darting hopes come hither stay awhile
In your very own home the land of despair
From azure vault to my demure tabernacle
Ensconced in the tiny but warm human heart
Pulsating with the irrepressible spirit of man
Come overwhelm the basin of make-believe

World is too beautiful for wars of denudation
Too fragile for conquest of dusky ideologies
Faith 'n fear are trappings of abstruse creeds
Rivet the feeble mind to exploding fantasies
Nurtured in ignorance and caprice in a world
Full of bleary eyed prognosticators voodoos
Religion is hypocrisy a distilled make-believe
Abject surrender to the cult of viscid thesis
It can scarce prevent the descent of wily men
Into a microbic inflation of cults and creeds
Pushing errant world into an unending ennui
Which nothing can refurbish nor ever rescue

Space-time twins are forever motion chimed
Their orderly gyrations resulting in creation
Man is left with nothing to lose except hope
Which lingers awhile till he is lured to sleep
A new man will arise for creation to proceed
Regain nature's trust to live within her means

Unlike him who wasn't cradled or soothsaid
Nestled in crèches nor bound to nursery cool
Lost to himself unfree and listless who flees
From superfluous parents teachers gendarmes
Society is useless for pursuit of far visions
Without running fountains of equity within

He needed mother's lullaby and father's hug
Feather touch of nurse when body was supple
He's awestruck society to him is insipid insane
Puts old homes on custom for bony progenitors
It's not the generation gap that separates them
But lust libido and fungous venal indiscretion

Society that doesn't see into child's dewy eyes
Hear music in his cackles who wasn't caressed
Who is reverentially colourful but not cuddled
Cruel destiny stares desert spread of itchy vice
That dries our emotions and the urge to strive
Time to usher in a new creed, calling attention:

That new man's descent rests on child's concern
Its for you me everyone to lay sound foundation
For every child to get mother's love father's hug
Attention by society benediction by our nations
A loved one is sure protection against disruption
Its not for nothing he is called the saviour of men

Rag-tag Patola

Tired sun is ambling down apologetically
Planets are placid not their original self
Our lovelorn moon is nowhere to be seen
Earth of course is left with a few mounds

The oceans are not navigable any more
Only Mansarovar has some water 'n fish
But Chins and Yaks nowhere to be seen
Patola is a lonely rag-tag mountain heap

The meek sun frowns over it for months on
Becoz earth's motions have slowed down
No body is recording revolutions anyway
Whirr of prayer wheel entered blackholes

What was once the Palk Strait was bridged
By a legendary hero searching for his wife
Hoping some day an Indian will discover it
If ever he failed in his enthralling epic search

Alas there are no Indians Tibetans Chinese
Albinos and Arabs or hare-brained tortoise
Because the earth is back to its original self
Without scars and exuberance of civilization

It's now smooth plain like the balance sheet
Of insolvent firm flattened by extravagance
Time has run-out nothing is left to scavenge
Maverick breed of men has long passed away

Temples of trinity capped by golden bells
Domes of cathedra spires piercing heavens
Forbidding houses of God or Statue of Liberty
Anything memory can recall is nowhere seen

On a rump jutting out of once sacred shrine
In the sanctum of flattened Patola, might be
A quaint glimmer of light struggles to glow
Sneering at lingering darkness in abiding hope

Tired mind is sick at failure to find an answer
To the gnawing quibble could world live longer
If man hadn't wasted resources on making queer
Grotesque structures turgid monuments 'n tombs

Its true hindsight reveals more than the foresight
Now at the terminal of our life's ultimate station
Humans you just can't do anything now but wait
For big bang to clear marks of human pestilence

Foundation of Civilization

Cultivate fresh olives and bury the bush fires
Fury of hostile elements set to destroy trees
Reared by mother nature to protect our tribes
From the ravages of blizzards floods 'n storms
Give us nearness, art of living, hearth 'n homes
Take us from land to land 'n across the oceans
In search of kinship 'n amity peace 'n oneness

Trees verily lay the foundations of our civilization
So banish wild growth and the pernicious weeds
Bush fires blaze to destroy source of human habitat
So let not poisonous weeds and wild oats to grow
Elements hostile to men ignite them for their profit
Add to miseries of creatures who keep us company
Trees tell us the secrets of living together amicably

So don't fell trees best friend of harassed humanity
Let not false tastes and designs dull our sensitivity

Priests, false script writers and quacks foregather
To pillage perennial wealth of hope love and piety
Banked in human hearts, to build their own castles
And let the Satan breach precincts of our conscience
Sectarian clerics mislead by pouting ill read canons
Secreted in golden caskets of human confrontation
Our future lies in living together not in contention

Not long ago sages said listen to voice within:
You cant survive without nod from creatures around
Fluttering hearts of sentinel trees clearing misty air
Hold water in their roots for crops 'n animals to live
Preventing mountains from disrupting 'n save our race
Chasten mighty rivers to follow their destined routes
So don't fell trees best friend of troubled humanity

Ashes of 20th Century

From densely burning pyre of 20th century
Ashes for the twenty first will be collected
By the loonies to assemble 'n cherish them
To sanitize monuments of near 'n dear ones
Build vastly better ones for their opulent God
Who however quitted before humans were born

Because He couldn't bear the nerdy company
Of those who revere the remains of their dead
Shun those not part of their cherished sect
But create heavens for their mutinous fancies
Hell for those living on pittance sans dignity
They will never ever learn the simple truth:

"Monologue of history recalls the vainglories
Vandalism 'n orgies of disembodied vampires
Century is a long enough time to remove traces
Of their blood spilled horrendous deadly deeds
From the annals of human quest to live in peace
Spark of awakening is all that's needed to do it

Centuries gone by unfold the lurid reality
Plush at the poles and swathed at the soles
Mankind is forever doomed since it calls
Fuss fads culture, piece of land all its own
Unless resets its compass of life to restore
God's kingdom of blessing or else face nemesis"

I've entertained God concept in life many times
I've felt He is part of breath coming 'n going
He is not distant nor even awkwardly different
Though not met him face to face I recognise Him
Sitting quitly at road end watching us pass by
He's embodiment of our soul face of our life

Bill of Inheritance

To you he is beautiful who is ugly from inside
He is sane who madly runs after fleeting fame
You have not known people both good 'n great
Proud pious bastion of morality charity 'n faith

In this make believe world of ever-changing hues
Shadows loom sense sulks light dims till gone
Civilization's pains produce prigs full of vanity
Mired in quicksand of ill-repute and larceny

Sanity's crow that caws all day is shooed away
Lewdness is well set at the bottom of holiness
Humans your life isn't only short but also shaky
You would never know when it parts company

Your tragedy is not that you die young or old
But what you seek in youth you get when old
What you crave for when old you lost in youth
To square the vicious circle is quite beyond you

Becoz you invoke destiny live by inheritance
Believe in mock heroics indulge in usurpation
So till you accept egalitarian human mandate
There isn't hope for you recalcitrant opiates

Wealth kept padded in chests of inheritance
Loses valence gathers sloth often ill-spent
Makes you satyric indolent mostly incompetent
Hoarded its a sure peril to your judgement

God Doesn't Believe in Inheritance

Crimes take place when the law sleeps
Law sleeps when the justice is absent
If justice is absent people make merry
Splurge and bulge on unearned money

Money a perky bug invented by thugs
Thugs do nothing only make profits
Profits avoid the honest who go to dogs
Dogs are loyal to beefy musky owners

Owners are gifted wealth in inheritance
Inheritance a theft in company by many
Rest denied inheritance by a sinful few
True, God doesn't believe in inheritance

Or else God sure won't be in existence
Succeeded by one unworthy of attention.
Crime 'n inheritance mate to spawn sin
A world full of larceny naked deception

Reason, God denied himself inheritance
So that wise men do not seek preference
Instead end savagery of rank nepotism
Which are marks of inequitable system

No good ever comes out of inheritance
Ugly remnant of vicious spiral of egos
Cosmos is premised on primordial laws
Of constant permutation 'n combination

Once without the burden of inheritance
You are heir to the kingdom of heaven
God seeks company of gentle persons
Unencumbered by worldly possessions

Good deeds to Inherit

Pray let us remain as simple beings
Full of hope and human aspirations
Live as comely humans and not scan
As godlings the riddle of existence

Forget the joy of skipping frontiers
We have no need for heavenly abode
Sans incandescence of humane souls
Pray heaven's gates be closed for us

May we then toil and sweat silently
Rise to realize gently the importance
Of creating less but preserving more
Lest the human spirit grows listless

As humans we have the confidence
Though in life we may beget death
Will sure leave good deeds to inherit
Our sole and the only prerogative

Stuff of Man

Man isn't what he is made of
Not just flesh bones and hair
There're much bigger things
In heaven earth he is made of

Mother's concern nature's feel
Many social mores good 'n evil
Help of dear ones seen unseen
Above all waves rising in mind

Which ain't flesh nor bones dry
Full of images dark and bright
Tall aside small stand sanitized
Man is reborn after every strife

Bravely straddling molten past
To see what future holds fast
To escape rigours of the present
Stride over bars put by heaven

Verily man is measure of values
The substance of restive history
Will survive escapades of ideology
As prejudice ends its waspy legacy

Conserve for Million Years

When soul talked to me I didn't listen
When I talked to the soul it declined
What is the point if there is no action
When I planned all my actions it said:

"What is the use, there is no vision
When I had vision it said mockingly
Horizon has receded and light is gone"

A human being, I didn't lose hope
Pursued it to reveal its antennae
To awaken me to pure knowledge
If we both are not the same entity

When I act or think it watches me
Is it an awakening seeded in future
Or else a self fulfilling prophecy

Turgid mind was eager to know about soul
As I've been seeing shadows in the dark
Heard music in bizarre silence of vacuum
Sprouts brooding in drought dry land

Agnostics debating if immortality of soul
Is not the challenge of human mind
To the treacherous finality of death

Guess soul permeates the entire universe
Has no size shape colour or any name
Resides in atom's belly gathers form
Wherein is stuck for a while off chance

Pale light intervened as if to admonish
Remember choicest blessings of your life
Are the limitations it imposes on itself

So I plan my present set in future
I know unknown is not my destiny
I commit no felony only seek grace
I think 'n wait count my blessings

There's enough for all our longings
Conserve you have million years to go
Sun and moon are our daily visitors

Computer Hug

Now you shouldn't worry about your many roles
Since the computer will do all your native chores
That is even sit by the silvery beaches and soar
And do all the pleasant things in murky settings
You would think of: covert love dance and sing

In time computer would forsooth grow of age
Want you to set it free from its cellular cage
Allow it to do this and that let it be anywhere
Indulge on its own, fornicate in ample sphere
Create its own breed faster than women dare

Weird rolling world full of comely computers
Would fain swell and soar on bouncy gliders
Live in pleasure in the succulent honey-combs
Messing lolling around will develop an intent
Indulge in concupiscence to their hearts content

Intent develops into an avid self-held manuscript
It has grown so fast from a babe to a bawdy brit
Now compues want all those holding bars fast torn
Between them 'n their progenitor the double born
Why can't them be free to the pleasure of a hug

Want to go beyond the timid sybaritic monosex
Pine for the company of sprite humans for sex
Only way to stem maddening compu explosion
Thwart compue-whore to produce not more than
A yummy vinegary broth in a flat frying pan

Let them not cross civilization's creaky gates
Humans are much harried by a worrisome fate
Left with little sense 'n vigour to decide in haste
Minds lulled by clutter of cybernetic think pad
Whether to go down drain of dark forebodings
Or reverse the gear stem madding compue spread

Tube-Mummy

You don't call me mom, just call me *tube*
You are not from me, though I own you
I care-take you thereby hangs a messy tale:
It gives me great honour if you are hailed
Gets me status as a woman of substance
Who carries mother's craft with success

Child sure you will go down to posterity
Not as a bastard but a notable post-script
To a daring woman managing as a man
With no femininity or private pendulum
As a wise madam, who created puppies
Sans humanity piety like computer chips

Which are not mended nor stored away
Instead microwaved to create a new world
Of stock, bargained at the printed price
Settled at legendry slippery market place
Where hell is cheap heaven out of fashion
Name fame for men with unctuous vision

Survival is the name of game for mute many
Hauling burden of venal unequal civic frame
If *tube* is tomorrow's fabled woman's name
Let this snooty civilization fade out soon
To save human kind from Satan's contagion
Spreading faster than the saner content in man

Chapter 4

Wanderlust of Thought

Uppity Fidgety Bug

What makes you call me un-ripped pesky atom
The twins in me are space and time pendulum
I myself am unaware of my mystic existence
But you proclaim to have scooped still deeper
Into my unlit core in immeasurable angstroms

I am just amused as you divine so wishfully
That universes are clobbered out of my debris
If that be true how does it explain any way
Their unceasing spread, increasing whirrs
You have no answers to my barmy enquiries

Your bagatelle digitally won't help explain
Exploding dark forces 'n rising black holes
Your hermetic space stations solar missions
Will only tell how aloof lonely and hapless
Earth looks from far above cowered in space
Even if you discover the cause of cosmos
You still remain mere mutating gene-moss
Thriving in feeble plasma of an aging earth
Your flesh is weak but your surrogate mind
Asserts, you go past the steely stellar limits

No, bother about rubbish in your courtyard
This beleaguered planet is your only abode
Even if you discover that there is yet another
With a diseased mind doddering old body
You wouldn't survive an eerie barren place

If you dare do it all in your little mindedness
Sure you won't ever last a single space-wreck
Credits of muzzy civilization notwithstanding
Learn to live well in your assigned habitat
It is coterminous with the rest of hot-spots

Go and mend alter stitch sew promote new
Legends of life to live in peace and harmony
Genes that humans are made of aren't feeble
They cover entire earth partnered by atoms
So regulate enhance the ways to prolong life

For, the denizens of the Earth like of which
There's none in entire burgeoning universe
We've lived a sheltered life in nature's lap
Occasional fracas but in perennial bonding
In mutuality which enhances our life spans

In the atoms navel are those stirring sperms
They don't mutate agitate unless hammered
If accelerated will've humanity shattered
So when signal is down making us quit
We will turn from matter into ageless spirit

Seer of Sort

I lurk in unseeing darkness uncertain
I am afraid of the lingering fuss of light
What'll I do with so much of it around
Only a niche in the heart to be illumined

        Light always cheated 'n deserted me
        I have discovered it is not genuine
        What everyone casually calls light
        Is a negation of sneaking darkness

Wilderness dungeons I make light of
If only my heart would guide me on
Am sure I will not be betrayed again
By charlatans, or quietly inveigle me

        Into the dimlit world of wry wisdom
        Which robbed me in heaven's name
        Of all happiness peace and simplicity
        And whatever little I had of humanity

I'm afraid of the enlightened ministry
Weird conjuring conspiring queer men
Living smugly in ornate holy homes
Hold fickle candles in God's citadels

Unaware there are many more regions
Not too far distanced but near at hand
Not even the heavenly light can expose
Only true endearing love can prise open

Now old, I intently look around to see
If I had left few pebbles on the tracks
For the little imps to pick up wondering
Gaily yelling someone deceived himself

Hugging tipsy beliefs in old unlit alleys
Of cobbled ideologies pussy vainglory
Ego blackening tales of scripted charity
Who won 'n lost is ill-judged by history

This small life has enough within to deify
If instead of gazing at yonder stars vaguely
We poured piety into our ample heartbeats
Sure no child would be without daily eats.

Wanderlust of Thought

These men crowded in old omni bus
Half comfortable and half monstrous
Irreverently plied from stop to stop
Many are the disparate callings theirs
Yet all seem to be moved uniformly

It's unimportant how 'n when they move
But what moves them skeptically along
They bare the skies 'n roughen the seas
To tend their wanderlust or Gods' design
No one ever cared, for it is unavailing

One day like flies they will be drawn in
By cryptic code carreering their lives
More inexorable than the Satan's guiles
Neither God nor men or Satan would know
Why destiny clipped hope's wings halfway

This pother and futility, roar and muse
Cruise into space, voyages across seas
Rollicking through earth aft and fore
Art forms and intricate culture designs
Surge of creation in stone extensive fine

Institutions rising on the ashes of the old
Loaded with exuberance of obsolescence
Civilization spreads, anon shrinks the man
Yet dares the space to peer into mysteries
To reduce God's sway to lone field formulae
Futile is wanderlust of thought 'n philosophy

Behold the murmur in the bowls of Earth
Fire under bed of seas gales dust in skies
More powerful than the handiwork of man
Hark not the erring mind but ageless spirit
Build not on the shifting sands of fantasy
But on the foundations of trust and charity

Pretty Earth is a poor cousin of galaxies
Don't scoop all its scarce treasures empty
There are no insurers and risks are high
Conserve all that's left for the vigil of life
On bedrock of virtues in the brooding night
Not to soar nor to simulate but to survive

Vibrating Universes

Oh me! I have discovered the ultimate reality, Brahma
The cause of all beings and the being of all the causes
Space seeded, time speeding, their travelogue is creation
Focused on mutation of ions incased in ninny atoms

Footloose galaxies have no manna, scope for polyploids
There is nary a thing at the centre of twirling biggies
Just the momentum caused by the voiding of space
Making vibrations, substance of many forms of creation

When 'n where it all began, time has its own limitations
To measure what begins at nothing ends in no nothing
Quizzing reality is that, the end is the new beginning
Tied to earth we can never fathom tapestry of universes

Until atoms we become beyond seizure of time 'n space
Ceaselessly mutating without apparent cause 'n effect
Cosmos is beyond the terminology of beginning 'n end
Creation is a progression of self-mutating endless forms

Synoptic mind thinks of Brahma fenced in time 'n space
Becoz that is the outreach of human's timid mind scope
To go beyond time space to fathom Brahma's universes
You will need to change genes to set out in outer space

Break all connections based on covenants of opposites
Thus freed from dualism of life 'n death light 'n darkness
Humans will transcend limits of convoluted ontology
Become free from thralldom of bogus feigned enquiry

Creation Hypothesized

A great seer tended to define
The source of all creation et al
Built a new algebraic equation
Adding a few powers on to it
Removing all imponderables

> In the end he was benighted
> Washed it all again hopefully
> Set out afresh to unravel it
> To build yet another equation
> To reveal mystery of creation

He just put one straight bar
At right angles to the other
Tried a third to join them both
At right angles to demonstrate
Thus was the advent of creation

> Rise of cosmos is premised on
> Law of Straight Bars put right
> To exclude the null hypothesis
> Some use these bars to ascend
> Others to descend to nether end

Those who descend said the seer
Strike the rock-bottom of truth
Who ascend have gods to rescue
Phew cried owner of lean donkey:

"We have nowhere to go to seek
Except into caverns of our beings
Creation is a cut and paste affair
Of Him who hurried in despair

To fill all nooks and the crannies
In space with all sorts of bagatelles
Mind held by the null hypothesis
Was left with little time to surmise

Why prate creation a big bang affair
No, it is a mad house God astride
All life forms are factored by time
There's so much for us to be satisfied

We aren't beyond hope and relief
Advent of creation is a non issue
The ones that affects us all alike
Is to ponder on right course and why

Nothing is gained in hurry burry
Life's gifts are for all and sundry
Sun moon alternate for one and all
Benign nature hates duality divide"

Apocalypse

World became overpopulated thru autism
Every space there was filled up to the brim
Even oceans were filled up by the humans
Tier upon tier like bees gadflies and worms

Many more crusts upon crusts were formed
For the tipsy gadflies to roam and gad about
Then those on the top, the recalcitrant opiates
Were battered bandied about by wind, storm

Those living unheard uncared at the bottom
Got crushed by turn and became base material
In long time past, like fossil fuels and quartz
Adamantine the substance of our civilizations

Humans piled sky high in pallid putrid heaps
Holding up clouds' free movements in skies
Dispersed they rained fiercely days on end
And when the Sun shone on windswept top

Soggy humans turned into dense vegetation
Which spread fast became denser over years
New depths and heights formed themselves
Rains collected here 'n there oceans evolved

A world in primordial beauty emerged anew
One cycle completed another to begin afresh.
Humans again grew corpulent filling space
Beyond the sun moons and teaming planets

Twirling in the echoing emptiness of space
At long last there was no space left empty
World of humans was forced to split again
Chunks hurtled afar in directionless frenzy

Across shrinking space expanding universe
World resumed shape free from wry humans
The hurtled units of humans retained nothing
Perforce changed form from matter to spirit

Turned into pools of calm coiled prescience
Amidst cosmic mutation human spirit pleaded:

"Save our minds to recall the blundering past
Enabled to feel the future even as ultima atom
Driven by the primordial laws of contiguity
Through the space with the stillness of speed
Till eternity bends, which won't be end though,
Only ruthless motion atop gooey thickness
Of the convoluted space-time confluence
Till their gyrations slow in their own slush"

Their slowing won't affect cosmic convolutions
Only blend eternity's varied disguised sameness
Into cosmic vacuity beyond human experience
It isn't worth measuring what process lies therein
Creation doesn't halt like great grumpy empires
Sputters as burnt out ash immutable and fine
Turns invisible matter, building blocks of universes.
And when vacuous space alters direction of time

New universes emerge, whirring across the space,
Human intellect, coiled power fuse, is active again
Bridging the past and the future in a new formulae
To continue its passion for abstract categorization

Life is short but conditioned by futile expectations
Knowledge porous destiny inked by provenance
To find what lies at the back of beyond is not sense
When where it terminates isn't in our competence

To ensure life on earth humans you reverse the gear
Shun haste bury venality and curry nature's favour
Beget trust learn to live in peace and contentment
With all life forms who give the humans sustenance

Amidst God and Satan

Why should there be pain at the place
Said to be the sure abode of lord God
If it is the God's Kingdom we live in
Why should there be so much of sin

The pain in my heart tells me mutely
God was conceived by Satan secretly
Who stuffed Him with million muscles
Bones restless run of blood 'n plasma

But Satan feared that He may germinate
Take shape call to attention his Creator
So he hurtled Him into the dingy valleys
Atop snowcapped mountains into space

Over oceans lands into sagging crevices
In fact everywhere he found piles of sloth
Confusion of dense vegetation fungi moss
Seething bacterial phenomena called life

Having set recurring seasons of change
For molecular forms of life to multiply
To turtle in pools of self consciousness
Satan returned to his anonymous fastness

Hoping to enjoy the Haven of quite bliss
He was disillusioned 'n looked askance
Becoz faith had ripped stolidity of beings
God had taken roots in Satan's nurseries

Accusing Him of impertinence 'n bad faith
And for lording over his domain ex parte
Berated Him for infecting human plasma
With equity, conscience and good sense

Amidst Satan 'n God life isn't worth living
Stretched thin on vanities of vacuous faiths
Indulgent child in man is still to come of age
Frolicking in wanderlust taking time to shape

To turn the earth into a Heaven of our own
Remove all distances 'n evil separating walls
Money is not a measure of man's enterprise
Continence not lust is the essence core of life

God isn't lured by temple bells nor by calls
Or by vain sacrifices penances undertaken
For the fully free and awakened man to arise
Got to turn the corner, veer more to the right

Soul Within Soul

The anguished screech of a lone crane
In the serene stretch of unbothered space
Revealed to me that there indeed dwells
A surrogate soul within the primal soul

The one is there for the being to endure
The other to appraise the wide world with
One is supplied with that free refreshing
Stream of blood 'n plasma from the heart

Other is punctuated by the brobdingnagian
Cares and concerns of life beyond relief.
Good sense virtues 'n values are slow footed
Vice windswept ego blind borne by hatred

Love is beyond the notion of time 'n space
Heart without it is a source of deeper ennui
To sustain civilization with love-lorn heart
Needing artificial respiration and transfusion
Is without merit a source of bloody friction

The insolvent being hurries not knowing
It is better to abide in the limitless love
Because pristine love is measured in eternity
And not one burnt by unchecked amorous glee

O soul! within the soul bestir end the duality
Of half life lived in vain 'n other in frivolity
Mere skeleton without flesh of human dignity
Humans steady your vision set right the compass
Rainbow of hope straddles the entire cosmos

Self Annulment: Moksha

For life's journey men have limited fuel
The power of their debilitating passions
Light of little stars to illumine their steps
Destination is far not mapped and unclear

Weary lonesome bereft of wit 'n direction
Lie marooned in dove cotes of civilization
They're momentarily deflected 'n forgetful
Rearranging scarce curios in slender design

Secreting their valuables in cagey niches
Ringed by cobwebs dust-laden 'n disused
They have long endured the burden of hope
Suffering mindless darts of neglect 'n wait

Built up philosophies myths and sciences
Institutions, cults creeds and tall shrines
To hasten life's tormented journey's end
To promised land of self annulment: ***moksha***

Civilization little abates life's unclear odyssey
What else does, they are not aware thereof
Of need should this pother go on unchecked
Trapped between time 'n its half bother space

There's no knowing when the perky twin elves
Free humans from the throes of birth and death
Travail of hate, soured love, mounting despair
Empty promises of hope, dry wells of charity

Time and space have same beginning and end
Because life's journey ends wherefrom it began
An intrepid gene will break chain of evolution
Dissipating font of life, spelling end of creation

Humans all that you can do to fulfill yourself
Live within nature's means persevere in peace
Replenish twice you take from nature's bins
Its the code to enhance life and ensure existence

Who Am I

I never say die, immortality is my basin
In bowers of bliss I grow in fulfillment

Day and night are woven into my breath
Mystery just a shroud covering my face

Winter rain or sunshine are same for me
Configuration of lines won't define me

Age passion reason wisdom don't soil me
In truth I am beyond the insolvent belief
Can you guess who am I: a solitary soul

Hope Dried in Roots

Austere ageless values not even for once
Linger in eerie vaults of frozen faith
They forsooth retire to the azure dome
Make-believe vain piety isn't for them

Splendid cathedrals with sky high spires
Touching gates of heaven alerting gods
The thousand pillar temples of trinity
Priests flush with vicarious authority

Dour faced slow footed vaguely aural
Pouting sermons from misread canons
Full of panegyrics causing confusion
Gullible are inveigled into submission

Who soar in high spirits lacking wisdom
White flakes of virtues condense in skies
Ill prospects of rain hopes dried in roots
Seek heavenly grace in painted wry faces

Million muscled man carries life in wraps
Trumped-up by those too close to deceive
Beseeches the unknown for brief reprieve
To make sense of life here, doom hereafter

Grim World of Make believe

I sleep dream and am adorned
I wake up and am bewildered
Is reality so ethereal bottomless

    Like crystal quartz it changes
    Undulates, turns in mind's mire
    Weird images dim all jumbled

It has no linkages with destiny
Nor with the luminosity of soul
Full of subterfuge and is illusory

    Berates mind and tames the spirit
    Rests on the dung heaps of pride
    Fuels misery pods of little men

It's brutal it makes us wake up
In the middle of benign sleep
To a grim world of make believe

    Life has taught me many things
    Foremost not to face the reality
    Which has many grim wily faces
    Each woebegone than the other

In hearts' corner there is a place
Called love gentle self effacing
Tender but strong enough to stand
Hate, puts aside fate, keeps awake

      Part of your conscience called truth
      Knows no pride, malice can't wean it
      From compassion, humane in content
      Needs just your unfailing attention

Has no foes knows no limitations
Increases as your trust accumulates
Needs no investment nor assurance
It's yours for asking knows no end

      Split the hair and you are nowhere
      Split the heart and you find it there
      Sure it's love that we all well know
      But in our busy-ness we just let it go.

Chapter 5

Return to your Roots

Humans Return To Your Roots

Trees shrubs meadows mountains deserts 'n oceans
Contain the simple secrets of the Earth the way it is
Don't scupper them to probe innards of far planets
If like earth they contain swamps cesspools of insects
Earth's the only live planet in entire girdle of cosmos
Don't seed lesser planets with miasma of your creeds

In the converging galaxies there are myriad bodies
Like Earth in the terminal cooling state of existence
Full of algae microbes mammoth horrendous mantis
But unsuited to rubric of life on our incredible Earth
With human slums in demystifying state of existence
In the senile phase of gadgetry replacing humans

Humans stick to your roots avoid the sinking space
Be here in the craggy clusters of myriad other beings
Conserve little that is left of life-enabling ingredients
May be you prolong the irrevocable decaying process
Thus carry withal pods of hope for ages more to come
Nature alone you can call yours preserved in space

Not whooping walloping supernovas 'n black holes
Much like our sacred Earth they have laws of their own
Our laws of chemistry or physics don't prevail there
Part of the cosmos though but different from ours
We humans have a special covenant with the Creator
Gifted with eternal soul, act as His eminence grise

May be as million years go by, as with your planet,
Some planets develop an ambience supporting life
While you're able to manage well Earth's systems
Maintaining its life supporting forms and features
And prolong your stay, as Earth retains its shape,
May you then plan an exodus to save human race

Noble Savage

Its time to return to the noble savage
Guess he is our destiny adorable fate
Never shed blood of dear 'n near ones
Ill treat women burden of gods envy

    Valiantly dared nature's dark dank forces
    Nor harmed neighbours or shed croc tears
    Never did he ill treat his beasts of burden
    Rose with sunrise and sang till sundown

As stars slyly appeared in the blueing sky
To give company to the sun-burnt moon
He slept on bed of pure honest pursuits
Of living 'n letting live in nature's midst

    I doubt he recognizes his petty progeny
    Men have frittered away nature's treasures
    They work to separate one from the other
    Stunned nature is alarmed for its own future

Quakes, holes in skies and aberrant seasons
It is nature's way to order us to court reason
We've to return to noble savage to escape ruin
Human life is a gift of nature that we live in

Gaia in Pains

I am the Mother Earth nobody asks me say
How I feel about all that goes on any way
For the sake of untested petty development
Humans you don't know what all is hidden
Inside deep chests of my varied wealth bins

Its not that I cannot push or restrain you
Its simply off putting, I just am hapless
Its so because you are part of my flesh
Even though I love this speck of a place
Which is part of the sprawling Universe

For millions of years I caressed it as mine
Given it shape and form, verdant terrains
Domains of glittering hues nowhere seen
Can't stop you, held by mother's remorse
Though it is dearer to me in all Universe

Denizens of earth forgive me my faux pas
True I nursed this nerd to protect you all
He turned my love sour little silly worm
Spent my meagre resources doting on him
It is painful now for me to pin him down

Has upset greening process beyond repair
Its beyond me to sustain his lewd tastes
He calls my life blood, plasma fossil fuel
Splits my soul in the pits of nuclear forge
Needs no oracle to say its time to reverse

He has aged and can't fix up another planet
His genes blood bones 'n senses are dated
Gaia's resources won't last him even a year
He will exist there as worm sans conscience
And without emotions just as a mere number

Earth in its infinite forms of life is coeval
But in his mad hurry to clear the ever elusive
Concerns of bending the shadows from afar
He may render this blessed earth desolate
And belie mother's instinct of absolution

I may yet pin him down to escape witless doom
Even if in shadow less expanse of rarified mass
He be the rarest gem in entire diadem, that is,
I fear, sans him God may neglect His ministry
My only hope, he regrets averts utter calamity

I Like The Earth The Way It Is

I like this motherly Earth the way it is
You can't tell the age of our relationship
By reading our faces or counting our ribs
We've ever been together the way we are
For ages gone by you nor I can remember

I mind your raring to the vulva of galaxies
To unravel the simple truth called nullity
If ever galaxies emerged as quartz or acuity
Bludgeoned by the twins of time and space
Reshaped by sweat of their furrowed brow

The flirty twins will swipe the galaxies off
Their blind elliptic and unceasing odysseys
Our relationship is beyond time and space
Has no limit as we are bonded in perpetuity
We've freed our horizon timid is the frontier

Earth puts on versatile garment of "nature"
Puts her sparks of life into our heart beats
Time 'n space fuse in vortex of our minds
Making us to outlast everything in cosmos
So let not Earth regret your galactic faux pas

Jungle Folks Are Humane

Child say not you are the father of man
I am the father that never was a child
I grew in wilds amidst hyenas 'n jackals
Eating legumes fruits and honey combs

In my own distant fiefdom none worries me
So long I enter not their forbidden territory
I dread not jungle folks nor crave their pie
Human world is crowded by people shady

Who practice larceny and usurp the rights
Of simple folks who serve them betimes
Their sordid creation in a distant Heaven
To dupe 'n terrorize credulous poor men

Who are forced into submission by touts
Jungle folks are artless open hearted free
Have no cravings for heaven, fear no hell
Are graceful ego free and ever so peaceful

Live in contentment and in beaming amity
City folks won't fit in our world of sanity
Shame you call our plain ways of life rustic
Becoz we eat to live which is not your wit

You are mean devour flora and fauna alike
Unmindful of things soiling your habitat
Will turn dear mother Earth into a hapless
Eerie sand spread, not fit even for insects

Everything in nature is tuned to a cause
You never bothered if you need a break
There's stock-taking even in the cosmos
Humans, time that you gathered your wits
To check if there is a better way to exist

Maverick Who

He guns because he has often been gunned
He lies becoz he has not been told the truth
He cheats because he's often been cheated
Doesn't speak truth becoz he knows it not
Religion he skips because it is about gods

He knows well he belongs not here or there
Becoz he has been poked by foul mouthed
Crafty wags spitting the pilfered verbiage
Lured by wily priests with yarns of myths
About heavens where roaches won't live

He knows not soul nor even resurrection
As well about there being a big cesspit
Of culture primed by dire hallucinations
Where razor sharp executants of myths
Push void plaints before the God almighty:

"To pardon all sinners, shun all the saints
Lest the Kingdom of Heaven be in jeopardy
From men of goodwill who preach loudly
Truth alone will triumph and not untruth
Leaving no scope for agents of falsehood"

He knows elites eat junk food roam wild
Afraid of light live in tall condominiums
Talk of human rights kill mute millions
Have dark faces eyes dusky mind tipsy
Invent lurid legends 'n talk of epiphany

A child of no fortune ever pelted by hope
Rejected by society, has no double lives
Dines in company of his kinfolks in places
Declared unfit under our municipal laws
He sweats for his keep and fears no gods
Lives gaily for the day future ground zero

To relieve earth of the crushing burden
Of desires rising in our scripted minds
Due to our insensitive treacherous mores
Restore to sacred child his divine rights
End his woes to revive hope for mankind
Or else be ready for destiny's cruel grind

Agnostics

Whoever baptized me *Philosophy* numbed
My wits and left me obese was a scoundrel.
Whoever spiked me to grimy back waters
Inveigled me to become the hand maiden
Of rakish characters caparisoned saints
Meanly called me *Religion* was a vandal

Never mind, whoever did it in half wit
I have put a lid on top of their pates
Made them grunt and groan pitifully
Wade in slush and slime lugubriously
Put them in the sepulcher of deep agony
And gored them to describe me *Ideology*

I am not at all pledged to monandry
I pair with whoever cares for a pastime
I break his will and put out his reason
Make him shadow figure pantomime
Forked tongued **scoundrels** 'n **vandals**
Both take a berth with me often times

Bewitched bemused they fret 'n fume
I full well make a dough of their kinds
Erelong they are out of their frisky prime
Jagged jaded juggernauts shrunk shaken
But the villain of them all is that pitiable
Brat uncouth unwashed peevish fellow

His rotund skull is differently structured
Never for a change has taken me for a ride
Vitriolic fearsome loathsome scum is he
Phew! yet I am inwardly drawn to him
He has a poise 'n a great crushing charm
Causes a gush and twitch in my bosom

Much tormented I dare not reach him
He will sure spew at me in rejection
He is cold boorish and awfully stern
Makes me suffer in pain and anguish
He nattily be-names himself **Agnostic**
He, I am sure, is not at all a simpleton

There is something in his countenance
Unmatched unsullied by time and tide
My worry is he outlives all of us three
When he is still in his youth lusty prime
He quietly weans away the child in man
Forsaken crest fallen damned all us three

I'd rather be interred in clammy dungeons
Next to the scraggy abominable dinosaurs
Than embalmed exposed to peering eyes
Jeering here lies the **Ideology** vixen of vice
Playfully fiendish visceral, a siren of sorts
With a rare capacity to seduce and vilify

Renegade civilization is humankind's lot
Dismissing pleasures of macho carnival
Lure of celestial heaven 'n the fear of hell
Prudish folks value-ridden vacuous vain
Roaming sublimated wilds of discretion
Will exhume remains of our civilization

Unravel scramble and consign all of us
To funerary dungeons of dark anonymity
What a cruel destiny for us maiden three
Fiddle faddle **philosophy religion ideology**
We served humankind for millennia many
Shaped their life culture romance 'n melody

Gave them value and quietly ushered them
Into an unmatched breathtaking civilization
Replete with revelry de-rigueur bacchanalia
Elixir of life with hope 'n promise of eternity
If the witless nerdy folks renounce them all
It is their clammy potion of fetid hemlock
Their awesome lurid fate not our requiem
Our heritage of totems tombs stays forever

Lest Celebrity Dies

Howling elite class spawned by high academia
Minds forever poaching on wetlands of fantasy
Tongue loose in slushy earthy elliptic verbiage
Provides them with a fattened ego vague mania

Waste their years bumbling in dim drowsy rooms
Hoping to recover lost years promenading malls
Masquerading as intellectuals in furtive dalliance
To climb commanding heights of social pretence

Surprised and belittled that myriads like them
Mulling mall of ambition sans credit 'n valence
Whose only claim to erudition is baptism of class
In high ornate domes of well articulated insolence
More unsuited to rubric of life the more pompous

Elite are bred to practice skulduggery 'n sophistry
They know not that beneath funerary halls of flurry
Lie vast reservoirs of nobility 'n nimbus innocence
Who don't proclaim their genius the touch of class
Unpretentious they aren't given to vain contentions

Elite are enabled to thrive on their loose knowledge
Proclaim their genius short of depth light 'n vision
Propound and mystify a sordid thistle of thought
Conjured up in masques of nifty vaporous erudition

Redeem learning from erratic extremism of expertise
Churned by patinated citadels of archaic academia
Order closure of mass education lest celebrity dies
Sophistry edges out ennobling radiance of wisdom

In knowledge society, set aside minds for research
To discover panaceas for numerous ills of our race
Rest groomed in basics to run the business of state
Its sin wasting time money on faceless baccalaureate

Intelligentsia

Hey! have you heard of Intelligentsia
Yes, beauteous bright looking creatures
Those who shun sensitivity of daylight
Lurk in places darkened by shadows
In company of kinsmen lacking insight

Create forms figures devoid of substance
Drab arcane and not worth their name
No better than the piles of smelly debris
Promoting waste of thickness of thought
Melting afore torching light of comment

They don't guide counsel but confabulate
Fudging images in the sanctum of dyspepsia
Spurred by impulsive and obtuse research
It doesn't enlighten nor touches the heart
But titillates causing cerebral fissures

Set off a ragtag flotilla of fatigued ships
In uncharted regions of brazen thought
Cruising across choppy waters just unfit
Unmindful of waste misery around them
Cocooned they are like any other vagrant

For six months they hibernate de rigueur
Spawning mules of thought in the next six
These purveyors of despair and lament
Are a brutal assault on sense and content
What purpose they serve at all I'm in a fix

Ensconced in the niche of idle thought
Fixated in myths cults sans originality
Spurred by inertia live by sweat of envy
Revel immersed in own vapid company
They're caricatures misfit in civil society.

Scholar of Eminence

Scholar of eminence knows little of ground reality
Forever soars in serene skies in maligned vanity
His perspective disappears in sudden obscurity
As clouds sodden with the sweat of confabulation
Turn ashy gray in moments of blighting thought

Ever like flurried bird with mysterious plumage
Mighty sweeps, grand strategies, striking twirls
Over lush green valleys full of blooming colours
But eyes as blinding flashlights of corporeal craze
Set on lowly crawling worms casually wrought

There's the joy of winter gone and the spring come
Air not lacerated by mist of congealed hypocrisy
Mingles with spirit of nature in gladdening bloom
What seeks he in the crowded woods of his moods
Sepulchral and decrepit as if all else was naught

Scholar of eminence gather your overblown folds
Life is just not a frail and a fast rubbishing parody
Tie the loose ends benign nature allows overdraft
Create new credits to set off old debts vainly piled
Salvage what's left to build stock for another life

"George Rags"

I slipped on a piece of crumpled paper
Coloured it was, had an address on it
George Rags, pax Britannica, care Delhi
Lodged it in nearby mailbox per custom
To reach it to it's avowed destination

In course of time leisurely unconcerned
It was back again on the self same spot
With the quaint inscription unclear on it
Addressee now resettled in Neuf Inde
Via Calcutta Madras 'n Bombay in turn

My troubles started and the search began

Nowhere was he found in Raisena Hill
Cantonment Marine Drive or Boulevards
Shiny interstices of commerce in culture
In hoary strongholds of outdated learning
Structured on corrosive baptism of class

Bedraggled domes of run down democracy
Board rooms of wheelers dealers and dons
Underworld serais slums all drew a blank
None of them likely places could boast of
Such a pedigreed one as the George Rags

An oracle of a sort whose scattered hair
Flowing beard with not a black dissenter
Declared: *A tribe is around a deserted hut*
Guess, it was he with his Indian cohorts
Has a book of Fowler guitar for company

On a mission to seize the spirit of nation
Even Empire's splendour couldn't summon
Has a glint in his eyes hope in his gestures
Glistening robes red hair and rye for repast
A mired breed of nation gives him company

Their gay abandon betrays spirit of rags
Makes them venal and wholly unworthy
Of the great country they claim as theirs
Waltzing boozing as if end's near at hand
Job done, George vanished, brood in snafu
Left with shredded souls 'n rags to mend"

Chapter 6

Encounter with God

Encounter with God

He sits in the seventh heaven all by Himself
Indulges merrily in the creation of universes
Followed by destruction apropos law of cosmos
Creating cyclical motion, our notion of eternity
Gives us a glimpse of His unmanifest reality
Nothing is hidden or unseen or beyond Him

Our seen rested on experience is unseemly
Our unseen is ignorance and shall for ever be
Life is short, memory shorter creating fissures
We can't retain much as we are porous within
Interior is shredded by sharp recriminations
Fueled by gooey self image jealousy delusion

All in all we're inane wrought in mortal frame
We create things that we can't for long sustain
Our imagination is fecund but highly implosive
A circular equation it shell never be squared up
We create our own gall and put God in there
As the dispenser of relief and things we desire

Verily we forever will remain misty distraught
Because resources of God being not unlimited
Desires rise like ripples in our scripted minds
The more obsessive salacious the more stifled
Those that get fulfilled leave us melancholy
Becoz we seek God in twinkling stars blue sky

Even if such a God be there as you declare
He has other ponderous concerns to take care
We can't be free from the locus of our being
The messy encasement of life of flesh 'n fluid
As we can't create our genome 'n environment
All our efforts result in fleeting achievements

To set our house in order we needn't replicate
To steer us clear of the burden of profligacy
We oughta make plenty of little that's around
And share it with any whosoever be deserving
Can't store for long we've such short shelf-life
Conserve not commerce for million years to go

Nothing will be restored nor even souls aglow
Earth's the only resort we've nowhere else to go
A premise we share with all the other creatures
Explore preserve life on earth the longer we can
For peace and collateral existence with all others
That's all we can afford now or ever here after

Odyssey Of Faith

"O! Brahmin where is the place
Most sacred, man should look to:

They abound in all His creation
But most sacred indeed is Kashi
Most ancient, laity and learned
In fullness of wisdom repair to

O! Bhikhu where is the place
Most sacred man should look to:

Indeed Gaya where the most pure
Got Nirvana thinking not of Him
But badgered beasts 'n humankind

O! Padre where is the place
Most sacred man should look to:

Bethlehem where Christ was born
To usher in brotherhood on earth
And redeem the wretched helots

O! Mullah where is the place
Most sacred man should look to:

Mecca where messenger of God
Made Caliphs to redeem infidels
Spread message of peace unto all

Why are these places sacred severally

Padre 'n Mullah say becoz no other is
Bhikhu, sameness of life echoes there
To Brahmin every other place is sacred
Where people sing glory of Almighty

Agnostic, why are you vain contumacious
Full of shallow vague quibbles unexplored

Becoz life is awfully short for ideologies
Wrapped in mystique far removed from men
Loathsome they are, boast about a panacea
For many moods and ills of miserable men

Their path is not a garden full of roses lilies
Marigold dahlias rows upon rows of daisies
Theirs a subterranean vault closed by walls
Lest unbelievers pollute, faithful turn vocal

For me all places are scared where people
Browse over history why men had gone crazy
Lust replaced love in man, dogma compassion
Humdrum dissonance replaced music of reason

Oracles ask men not to see through mind's eye
But hark blissful promptings of your own heart
Issuing soulful music and rainbow of mercies
Not elegy cascading from old sodden scriptures

To repair to holy places to pray isn't in my mood
I search why sacred places don't beckon one 'n all
To me the smile on child's angelic face is ecstasy
Eating with her his two tiny hands dearest bounty

Her his today unsoiled, tomorrow not uncertain
Is a dearest spectacle speaking of high heavens
If your hoary Gods ensure they will not shed tears
Nor will ever suffer painful neglect and privation

I will be fulfilled beyond all pooja mass or namaz
And shall sweat to secure for the blessed children
Sojourn free from fear hunger 'n meddlesome men
Pleasant stay in earthy heaven presided by humans

Where none will claim God's exclusive attention
Live without the burden of Satanic inheritance
A pleasant abode of God within our competence
Yes, indeed if soul of child is saved from demons

Fuzzy Faith

Civilization distances culture constricts religion divides
Fuzzy faith grows slyly out of decrepit befuddled mind
But not from the sweat of human brow or from hearty dew
Faith is befriended both by culture half brother civilization
To drag meek humans to a divided acrid acidic existence

All of three perpetuate fissures in the human conscience
Enabling but the sinful few to lord it over, like pestilence
And the rest of mute faceless masses pure of hearts, docile
Are kept under the fuzzy vacuous beliefs by all the three

Drown all the pixy three in large sacred pool of humanity
So that human beings are freed from the curse of villainy
Of feisty religion culture civilization abetting repression
To remain free, humans have to banish all of them three

Faiths may be good, faithfuls better, faithlessness is best
Sitting on edge of earth thinking of far heavens is worst
Mind can't survive on ration of hope nor spirit on illusion
Neighbourliness is good peace prevails love not hate lasts

How can sins committed in murky business or over pulpit
By the sleight of hands or on the fast tracks of ill repute
Be reprieved by God on doomsday when only the sinful rise
To be sent back to itchy suppurating world of sin 'n strife

Live this chancy life well, be unbothered of hell or heaven
Stop the currency of religion to hypothecate human souls
By rhapsodizing archaic sermons corrupting naïve humanity
Sure humanity will then arise free from all the slush of envy

Sanitized Buddhas

Prince of Peace the preceptor of ahimsa
Got enlightened under a verdant Banyan
Roots hanging from its radiant branches
Its glistening leaves radiated noble ideas
Now Banyan stands in splendid isolation
Revered for its historicity not inspiration

Legacy of Banyan is more momentous
Its fluttering leaves pulsed the message
Of relevance of men animals and trees
Humanity be freed from malice 'n greed
Misery is due to absence of right vision
So righteousness be your raison d'etre

The famed Banyan will not be around
Only consecrated Buddhas will abound
The cry of Buddham Saranam Gachami
Uttered through dense curled upper lip
Transmitted through the captive tongue
Won't echo the concerns of human heart

Renounced his empire gave it in charity
Took to robes went door to door for alms
To banish sly ego, the supreme conspirator
Talked of middle path, eight vows to follow
Wanted to turn rigged world upside down
Usher in human spring, a new civilization

Crop of humans nurtured in trust, right
No scope for gerrymandering or genuflection
A basket full of blessings for one and all
Leaving no room for grabs or sequestration
Nobody usurps or hoards for inheritance
Alas! seed bed yet unready for enlightenment

Christ in Frame

Prithee don't put me in the small frame
It is not large enough it hoodwinks me
Limits spread of my persona and depth
Promotes banality hides oases of faith

People cast glances forget my pains
Me put in the frame my spirit is gone
Form gathers but meaning subsides
Makes mockery of Christ otherwise

Virtues and vices are placed together
Making botched up humans to ponder
Is Christ unframed understood better
Or framed christened in mystic letters

Don't carry cross to smother his image
He lives in hearts of all, good men 'n bad
To see Him you need self-purification
Misdeeds are not absolved by sermons

You don't see Him whom I see every day
Cornered on the margins of lonely streets
He eats but rarely whatever is offered
Taunt 'n neglect affect or hurt Him not

He suffers for us to clear dense woods
Covered by miasma of greed and treachery
He is ubiquitous Him we must endear
To stave off doomsday that seems near.

Jiddu : Unwilling Prophet

Ye beseech me: "I be God's angle"
Who lives in the distant heaven
Presides over time but is past time
Gets your daybreak hauls nightfall
Hopes happiness dreams 'n desires
Rendered comely by His holy grace

>Creates all living beings like dolls
>Who would never know their creator
>Surely such a God never existed
>Who you mouthed in your infancy
>Begad! I'll never be His angle one
>Nor ever like to dwell in His heaven

Many things happen to you by proxy
Unprovided nor wished otherwise
Yet you endure in viscid delusion
Witless vain self-seeking 'n sinful
You attribute your curses to Him
What He loves is spurned by you

>Yet you beg I be God's angle to you
>What insensitivity and caged mime
>You won't be graced timid you are
>Those pure at heart seek not God
>In legendry and vapid incantations
>Nor in doomsday or at redemption

Crazy you are lured by false visions
Making my beloved motherly earth
Pestilential place unfit for us humans
Jettison old ideas harbouring fallacy
Self-seeking prized as self abnegation
Don't seek in machines your salvation

    Let progress bespeak of human compassion
    Affirm man's raison d'e tre peace and amity
    Nor commerce ever choke your conscience
    The balance sheet of life has no debit entry
    All prophets are the rare gifts of the Devine
    Revere them as one from whatever clime

Airy Fairy Hypocrisy

O! religion faith who faked you in prehistory
When man wasn't a savage truly human was he
Roamed the wilds unhurried for victuals to live
For the day, not bothered if there tomorrow be

Gathered nature's plums and sat under open sky
Pooled them for hearty meal in folksy company
Moved from one place to another in wide space
But claimed no territory as his exclusive place

To fight for food or for land available in plenty
Was not in his vocabulary nor was fenced by ego
His future was uncluttered by the burden of past
Nor did he store or built battlements in distrust

Little did he cavil if there Garden of Eden be
Or skyscrapers huge mansions roaring highways
Space stations to peer deep into high heavens
He knew he has to live by the sweat of his brow
Dough of charity sans forgery of waspy legacy
Which burdens the mind betrays to conscience

O ! religion you have made him crave for things
He never dreamt nor ever considered as worthy
All unsuited to his folksy life and native genius
Heaven, you conspired to choke his conscience
To smother his soul, fill mind with dissensions
His idyllic fief is not same since your intrusion

He moved accompanying Sun from East to West
Beholden to the Moon ever new glorious sunset
Blessed, woke up at dawn as sparkling dews drop
Buds open and the birds chirp announcing peace
There won't be any regret amongst his tribesmen
Faith if you retreated to your airy-fairy hypocrisy

God Has His Own Worries

I created the universes for Me to survive
Braced by hell and heaven in space wide
I sought company of noble 'n pure people
Simple trouble free may be not so eventful
Put them with Me in My abode of Heaven

      People in the hell are more resourceful
      Those in heaven are not resource-wise
      Conscience sticking out mind obtruding
      Holding them from doing anything useful
      Erelong resources of My heaven depleted

As I neglected My universes they started
De-shaping, black holes, cesspit of galaxies
Emerged, universes speeding farther away
Thereby weakening My hold on creation
Making Me more unpredictable uncertain

      Staid serenity of earth's seasons changed
      Universes headed to where I don't belong
      To collide before I can call them back home
      May well spin off to a dull revolving rotund
      Mass of un-depleting mound of nuclear ash

I may yet reorder My gravitas 'n pace anon
Bunching all loops of My placid presence
To create balance sameness 'n order around
May be first I turn the earth into a vast forge
Of benevolent actors fair active to depend on

Making highly recumbent mass of humanity
With inherited nobility to leaven the dough
Of creativity to garner resources for a new life
And let Heaven not bear their undue burden
Not so opulent a creator can bear much longer

In truth I did not create man in My image
With a stony heart 'n ego ensconced therein
Living on strongly bursting pile of hatred
Not of My making, a genre of his own kind
Even as I couldn't while black holes emerged

Even I wish, I can't change laws of mutation
Framed even before hell 'n heaven were born
Even the black holes in My loop of creation
Will take primordial form after dissolution
Humans, I worry you'll be your own ransom

Methinks, this puny man can very well survive
Monstrosities of his mind speech and actions
Decides to retrace his steps to Garden of Eden
Properly clothed and suitably trained to discern
Else, he sure will follow the dreaded dinosaurs

Folksy Religion

Religion it was told to me is uplifting
Pathway to godhood abode of divinity
Life of piety peace and fulsome bliss
World of compassion noble and pure
Knows no boundary in land or sphere

      I roamed in dales valleys pastures green
      Across dense forests 'n high mountains
      Befriended simple folks mending fields
      Merry shepherds tending herds amidst
      Slim trees lush green grassy silky slopes

The bedouins in the dry itchy deserts
Teetering their camels to oases of hope
Fishermen in their dingy catamarans
They know little of religion or of gods
It's their daily catch they all worship

      Cut into fine pieces pray and eat it
      Thank the high heavens, the vast seas
      For daily replenishing their ample repast
      And are unmoved by huge domes of piety
      Their god's simple, religion no obscurity

They hang their gods atop sentinel trees
Crests of waves or misty mountain lairs
Live under shadow of their homely gods
They know no hunger ill-fame or rapine
Divine decree or even immaculate mime

Simple endeavour brings manna aplenty
Don't need cities nor lush market malls
Brimming with faceless sundry people
They don't fudge their beliefs mulishly
Mercy, Satan hasn't turned them puritans

Double Face Of Religion

Why should I repair to religion
What has it done for me in sum
Except confuse, place my destiny
In hands of an unknown entity

       Not to question unctuous tenets
       Someone in remote putrid history
       Touted in moments of vainglory
       Not concerned with my drudgery

Put me in slough of despondency
Failed to render me any protection
From necromancy or livid heresy
Ate all my vitals made me drowsy

       Pain 'n poison lent by cruel clergy
       Calls it lord's wish in sheer guile
       Deigns me to just endure His mercy
       Abhorrent pitiless endless agony

Take away religion its double face
Resurrect the noble savage in me
Nature shaped in millennia many
Lived in collateral peace harmony

       Roamed the wilds in search of food
       Enough for the day and not to store
       Sang his heart out in nature's midst
       Was kind to neighbours and beasts

Heaven A Cruel Joke

Hell where is your venomous sting
Heaven your hyped parlour of porn
My soul is entwined in knotted life
The journey is long little tired I am

> Destiny I cavil not nor morals swish
> Salacious pleasures not a joy for life
> They are placed betwixt hell 'n heaven
> Seeking them we end in Gehenna anon

Heaven O! fool is a cryptic cruel joke
A lump in the brain spins lurid desires
Remain unfulfilled becoz those near you
Conspired to seek more than their due

> Hell and heaven beguile to spin ironies
> Life is not so dull nature truly is benign
> We'll live free if heaven 'n hell collide
> In Eden Garden, Adam Eve will rejoice

Freedom From Irreverence

O faith through dense vales, glens and dales
Meadows ravines deserts and the vast oceans
You took me to the heights 'n deep into space
Consecrated places sacred though not to all
To discover the God's abode His famed citadel

Tutored me to say His prayers in uniformity
Pictured to me that heaven's reserved for me
Hell will be theirs who pray not in conformity
Now at cross-roads of life I see neither light
Nor reason to discover your god at others' cost

Mutter His prayers but denounce others' gods
Create world of disdain hate where there's none
Faith high curse be on you I was lured to infamy
Away from naturalness and romance of colours

My people roamed free in their own native terrains
Rivers flowed to water crops 'n vegetation aplenty
For all creatures and for men to set up granaries
Lest mankind starve when like hell its dusty dry

O faith you have polluted my neighbourhood
Punctured my soul knocked out gullible mind
Its now time that we put out the lightening bug
It has created dreaded darkness spread falsehood

Makes it hard for us to live in collateral peace
Faith reared in fear and abuse we don't need
It's freedom from irreverence and venal creed
That we need to scale heights of human dignity

Impenitent Crusader

I will not miss your God at all any time
Age after age I will be born human free
In kindred company with streak of pride
Never abandon love for all fellow beings

      I don't care if your God dares to purge me
      I've lived full life every pulsating moment
      Hated the soothsayers forked tongued saints
      Who singe the gullible with threat of hell

Little do I care, for His threats don't prevail
A self perpetuating ally of voodoos is He
Dwells in dark dens visited by the guilty
Neglects them who sweat to earn their keep

      How many times you ruined in His name
      Treasures of human excellence and wit
      Destroyed vast wealth of arts and crafts
      Buried civilizations acme of excellence

Your lust for human blood doesn't abate
Orgies blood baths and hurried funerals
You always justified them as His mandate
Horrendous tell-tales of history bare it all

      Curse be on such a God who quietly lets
      Pontiffs conspire to order man-slaughter
      Of non-conforming sceptics and dissenters
      Lest the name of stand-easy God is sullied

Smoking the dim-wit heathens for heresies
Their forebears muttered to their hoary Gods
O! ghoulish peddlers of hate 'n mock God
You mutilate Him who dwells in human form

       There's no place for you here or anywhere
       You will be hounded like vermin forever
       Wherever humans dwell and nurse many
       Wounds inflicted in the name of divinity

Crusaders egged by knaves 'n charlatans
Rob the humans of their sanity unabashed
Commit crimes even Satan won't envisage
Your savagery has left nothing to salvage

       Sins you committed to please your Gods
       Are beyond the scope of our humane laws
       In our just laws, meant for comely humans
       No punishment is enough for such of you
       Your chapter of hate 'n felony is over now

Non-Believer Skunks

O Padre! O Caliph! where is your God absolute
Who allows killings of pagans kafirs skeptics
Nay all unbelievers in what you passionately say
If atheists pagans have no place in your heaven
Why did then your lord God create them anyway

Why the faithful, to extend His undisputed sway
Rip open the lives even of women and children
Why ever then God almighty lord of all the heavens
Space and time and the unceasing creation withal
Created these skunks, the nonbeings dissenters all

Why did He not implant in their infant minds
The seedy instinct to follow the God you adore
Who is not embedded in their own native lore
But is so different awesome ever more distant
Even though He may have nectar myrrh galore

You want pagan's creed culture art 'n history
Cast into gehenna contaminated by Satan as if
Let your God appear with flowers in one hand
Love and mercy for all the humans in the other
Compassion in eyes, full of grace in kindly heart

Pagans kafirs and dissenters all will be praying
To your God absolute without plaint and prying
Place Him amidst their Gods of ancient regime
Worship Him as one of their own till eternity
Herald peace and shower love on everybody

As a child I was head over heals in love with God
Into my adolescence I became staid indifferent
Now having lived life with all its changes 'n chances
I've realised how utterly useless indeed is He
For a life of virtue vice or peaceful existence

Gods Descended in Hordes

We consigned our gods to their Heaven
So that they let us humans live in peace
In company of our kindred country folks
In woods and dales, glen and meadows
Worked by dew 'n feted by efflorescence

      Erelong gods sought company of humans
      Share their banality thrive on their pains
      Even before we could say no to the Gods
      They lodged themselves in the suburbs
      Of the human heart slyly in total apathy

Our noes were treated with loud guffaws
We are lesser souls want to be left alone
Free to reap our harvest of sin 'n shame
Face destiny without awe of retribution
We know fate 'n karma are excuses lame

      They descended on us in unruly hordes
      Destroyed our peaceful hearths 'n homes
      Had churches built where our corns grew
      Morphed the hills for temple bells to ring
      Each more majestic than the hovels of men

We're made to creep in abject obeisance
For relief of god-sponsored pain 'n misery
Betrayed by deceit and craft and witchery
We won't survive if Gods are not leashed
Put away in conclaves to dwell on their own

> It is in fear of them that we kill our tribes
> Sing psalms 'n paean of praise unrequited
> Commit deeds even demons indeed shirked
> Erelong, they made hell of our blessed earth
> Duped us to a life of doom before doomsday

I daresay we will never ever have a Heaven
On our earth if Gods have one of their own
We will never have peace nor brotherhood
Until Gods are returned to their own abode
And we regain our conscience humanhood

Beyond Redemption

Gods descended on earth to lesson the burden of heaven
It is the place where they admit on subtle discrimination
Those who have reneged their faith in human discernment
Dulled self-esteem morphed their conscience for pigment

It has been a fudged duel of dissent between man and God
For ascendancy of sense and reason over jejune thoughts
Never did man face Gods in such an ugly and uppity form
Who admit into their heaven people only on servile norms

Gods have burdened the hapless earth beyond redemption
Full of those nothing in common except self adulation
Forgery called faith, faked Gods of incomprehensible forms
To threaten wise dissenters with gehenna fire of dissolution

Now there's no place left in Heaven for men of conscience
Who crowd shanties ghettos downtown rag-pack slums
Who have challenged Gods to let them mind their business
Certainly the Gods couldn't have made blessed earth worse

Henceforth only they will survive having much in common
With folksy humans who live by the sweat of their brow
The writing on the wall says simple folks in human casts
Will outlast stars galaxies black holes all that is in motion
Becoz humankind are on the mast of flagship of creation

Don't Stun My Conscience

Faith why do you stun my conscience
It remained serene for ages I was born
Was full of the essence of compassion

>Faith you've slyly entered my precincts
>Polluted my mind, ravaged my feelings
>Irretrievably have warped my perceptions

Carved blind spots inside my vision
Lacerated my world with ring worms
Of many alternating hues dark brown

>O faith you have no faith of your own
>Or else you should not have spawned
>Sinners and saints to spread confusion

You've ravished all virtues and values
Humans aren't safe in your shifty hands
Mired as they are in renegade history

>Tyrants and goons have safe Heaven
>Gresham's gift to man is ever in action
>Currency of faith replaced God in man

Numbers don't betoken vibrant wisdom
Nor assure a place in the yonder Heaven
Whose walls are tiled with vengeance

>O faith take away that ravenous virus
>Of heaven and hell from our vocabulary
>Here's enough for all if you leave us free

Muggy Concept of God

I encountered God in quiet contemplation
I couldn't believe at all He could be so wily
Mean dotty and like me always on the sly
Warns of consequences if prayer missed
With prospects of slithery hell let loose

I kept commitments as father 'n husband
Left no time for mass or prayer thereafter
Yet I was grilled berated for blasphemy
For neglecting prayers to creator of cosmos
Who gives to all bounties graces as He does

In long arduous journey humans have learnt
Justice harmony are milked by human touch
There is nothing to fear at all if you harbour
Humanity in your heart minds are kept free
Nature cloned you as best in millennia many

So be not swayed by muggy concept of God
He has many things to manage in His spheres
Stocktaking chomping chopping redundance
Creating humans He ensured His continuance
Now mandates, you manage your own affairs

God Missed in Birth and Death

God I missed you awfully when I was born
I missed you again when eretime I was tombed
All through my life though you're by my side
You never cared whether I was dead or alive

>   Visited every church with lavish gifts I vied
>   For ages past I did it though unreason wise
>   Unaware what all I was staking for heresies
>   Dried up hopes and expectations un-arrived

I was put in the nursery of faith sense receded
Learnt how to hate and not to love otherwise
Show concern for others in lingo of purple lies
Discernment 'n trust dubbed errant nonsense

>   I have lost count of ages since hate arrived
>   Killed fellow beings blessed by other Gods
>   More they cried more I vied to annihilate
>   Bloated clergy promising heaven as prize

How long this madness shall haunt the fate
Of those with reason not tide on their side
I don't want to lose many hued civilizations
History's copious accounts of glory 'n gains

>   God if you can, save me from my kith 'n kin
>   In wolf's skin with little sense 'n multiple pride
>   Frenetic faith chokes, dries up fonts of reason
>   If it goes on unchecked only ashes will abide
>   It's up to us now to stall faith rescue mankind

Death A Fulfillment

O death don't leave me now as I need you most
You have been around me in thick and thin of life
You chaperoned me, guided my footsteps small
From infancy to childhood to valour in manhood
Through the vineyards of faith to citadels of fame

You charted my journey with signposts of hope
Success secured through moments of fervid strife
Wisely beckoned me to follow footfalls of destiny
Made me to endure many upsets 'n darts of villainy
Of mealy mouthed foes dressed in friends' guise

My sojourn on earth made bearable purpose wise
Despite occupational bitterness pain 'n many strifes
Now having lived it with all the changes 'n chances
Self-assured fulfilling on time life's many errands
Without you life wouldn't have been meaningful

Stay awhile as I settle my credits and many debits
Incurred because of the venality of morbid praxis
Pillaged by dwarfs lording as pompous celebrities
Whom the visionary in me nor people could undo
Nature will no doubt take stock of their perfidies

Death I'll ask you to leave my company betimes
As chimes of bells from nether world are heard
Destiny expelled roles sanctioned by law finished
Assigned jobs done to render to society its due
Life rendered solvent, death will be a fulfilment

You kept my company when I was hail 'n hearty
Why accompany me now, I have done all my dos
Is it, I am a pious compliant being, a dear soul
So even I am all set to say *finish* you want to stay
Well, I'll wait till you find another soul on the way

Conscience Astride

O! death why are you taking time to come
Have I still to do something left undone
I've done everything I thought was right
Except that I didn't keep my money tight

I have my values 'n compassion in place
Conscience has been my indomitable guide
I've incurred no debts, amassed no wealth
Ensured mind 'n heart are in same breath

Harked liberating spirit not spotty mind
Body has aged but spirit to serve is alive
Death no scare if your scoreboard is clean
Life a bed of roses with conscience astride

Wounds Deep Under Dogmas Skin

O spirit heal my wounds hidden deep under dogmas skin
Walk the faith with me lacerated by verbiage of vain ideas
Escort me at cross-roads where endless pedestrian egos
Choke the few bumpy roads forking to the no man's land

Counsel me when forests are burning rivers are drying up
Heaps of grains stored to stave off hunger rot turn fungous
O spirit stoke the sedate God ensconced in the human hearts
Stir the sunny conscience lying comatose there for ages inert

Putrid history has no true record to recount its misdeeds
Except when rare visionaries mused to chasten humanity
Evil ones calling compost heap of jargons advent of sanity
Festoons buntings flutter alike atop villas of saints skunks

Who legislate, charge humans of sins committed in proxy
The meek, pure of heart forced to bear lifelong drudgery
Atoning sins wily clerics made them commit gratuitously
Who drain the human mind of all desires to live amicably

Faith fattened by feisty dogma muzzles human conscience
Stuns the mind bleeds the human heart of pity and empathy
If at all it has done any good to gentle artless human beings
Is to install flasehood spread myths subverting truth 'n piety

Its dogma that prevents humans to come out of their infancy
Crushes noble human aspirations to live in peace and amity
Rare is the saint who insists love alone triumphs not hatred
There is scope enough to tone down self to avoid regret

I cry for Religion

I do not decry religion I only cry for it
It has sunk so low that wit just abhors it
Questions its errant myths and heresies
Its make-believe affirmations lack piety

It vitiates the jest for life and liberty
Degenerates into a formidable scowl
Ignores the charm of human continent
Sermons have ritualised insolence

Puts a full stop to the search for truth
Savours thoughts uttered in antiquity
To fault the design of manifest reality
Uses myths to explain random events

Promotes lores of ancestors as charms
Holds hope and promises resurrection:
Patriarch's sane advice is to bear with it
As souvenir of gusty mind's excursion

It's full of the tales of cerebral ideation
Malignant appendix needing attention
Causes mental gush that invokes insanity
Occludes reason and promotes absurdity

To rope in religion groom the conscience
Road to peace amity is through patience
Heaven isn't there it is very much here
If you take care share 'n act with reason

It is about God

Don't talk of religion it is about God
Becoz He is not in our daily business
He is concerned with hell and heaven
So talk it when heaven not hell is near

       Religion is an impostor vulgar verbose
       Only good about it makes us comatose
       Centuries to recover from an overdose
       Ministered by stargazing lachrymose

Leave religion aside sit down 'n listen
Business of making money faster than
That intrepid guy who doesn't fear fall
Has vigour more than the vision he hauls

       But there are many rocked by religion
       Passive damn duds with no eyes 'n nose
       Unable to smell sweet breeze that blows
       Around people fulfilling humane goals

Higgledy Piggledy Mutt

You read nothing since you earned just a farthing
You worshiped none because you followed only one
God is a vernal shadow of man's many aspirations
Man is natures gift to itself unmatched and eternal
Clothed in virtuous beliefs, guided by conscience

Shun all those beliefs not having man in center
Eschew all thoughts which have no love in them
Forbid those actions which are not service driven
Ensure always on top of your thoughts 'n actions
Are the smiling faces of genuine virtuous men

Seek no vapid pleasure creating human deprivation
See every penny is spent to enrich the human content
End this higgledy piggledy of making dumb money
Recover lost ground you are so close to perdition
You don't need a Jeremiah to return you to reason

Scalar Myths

When shoddy myths become fierce Gods faint
Humans soon turn to lock their treasured gains
Lest sacred knowledge is scattered on ground
Wicked ones become wiser than the humans

        It all began quietly in the nascent human mind
        Why all dreams occur with so much of sequence
        Do they project our past or predict the future
        Why make sense only when we are in slumber

Humans had lived free like the birds in high
Sang lilting melodies atop their pure hearts
Had no enemies ate and drank off nature free
Roamed the wilds followed sun 'n the moon

        Sat by the side of glittering river in ripples
        Saw the big fish eat small and shark sharks
        Plunged into the river swam to other side
        Spared, as there was no blood on his stride

Moved freely in wilds with beasts of prey
Hare 'n hounds deer 'n dove all unscarred
Peacocks parrots mynas scampered along
Kept company entered not in their frays

A gay jungle fowl that turned sky round
Made friends with men laid golden eggs
Chicks came grew flew into forest wide
Mad ape in man secreted one killed ate it

Blood smeared hands eyes red, distracted
Was flustered having lost golden crested
Sense palsied greed has fused into craze
Tears apart maiden hen in sickening rage

Thence frustrated men are in terrible bind
Smother every moving living thing around
Even their likeness to calm feverish minds
Yet are unable to extricate from original sin

Now unsafe amidst their own fellow men
Full of spiralling blind hate flawed vision
Imploring airy myths to perpetuate fetishism
Instinct of survival may yet restore reason

Insect Mind

Lord God make me a lonely insect
All of a short life with just a spirit
Little light and refreshing breeze
I seek in your world of many hues

Gather me then back to your fold
Not to return to your blissful hold
I know better be an insect not a man
Surely not fashioned in your image

Claims eternity has freak provenance
Has fickle mind ever changing dreams
My insect mind is jaded and crusty
Lord God give me just the plain sense

To hop here and drop there in sprint
Fitful delight is all I seek not eternity
Men 'n insects have no place in heaven
Reserved for them not insects nor men

Walk as Zombies in Fear

Its pity God has been used misused 'n abused
And made to tell the truth or lies as you liked
To anoint and grace villains vandals voodoos
Didn't bother silly things you made Him do

You made Him ordain niggardly as emperors
Sanitized cellar walls making sinful to pray
You made Him do anything that's so ungodly
He looks askance having spent His all on you

He reduced the universe into earthy module
For you to keep His trust 'n ensure its tenure
God may relent but this turgid lump of flesh
Can't escape nature's laws for irreverence

Squalls high-tides, quakes and ozone holes
Have taken things beyond anyone to ignore
Unless you alter your stance reverse the gear
Amidst debris you'll walk as zombies in fear

Chapter 7

Bulls & Bears

Bulls & Bears

What business is it that trades in bubbles
Counts profits when prices are in troubles
Hedges chips and dips when in deep fray
Runs with the booty when it is time to stay

What kind of place is this crowded bourse
Frequented by the well fed bulls and bears
Everyone is crazy sharing pushing bullshit
But as the bear straddles all cave into pits

My feeble mind can't divine why bourses
Called sinews sources of nations surplus
Change their mood like feeble weathercock
The moment even a fickle westerly blows

There are tides in affairs of men 'n women
The neap and spring in the bosom of oceans
What kinda tides create booms 'n tail spins
Blowing the heads 'n chopping the bottoms

Goddess of fortune visited every home
Now you've caged her in corporate grind
Countries rise 'n fall when capital squirms
People get cheated when business is prime

People aren't judged by how many stocks
They hold like perfumes in golden caskets
Their sweet scent of human capital locked
In over valued scrips kept in reed baskets

When bids and bets aren't made to acquire
Legitimacy in sphere full of unearned lucre
Guns will go silent 'n businessmen won't aspire
To make money at the carnivals on the sly

Blessed is Money if it Reaches Many

Why to make money just for its own sake
Makes you do business in the dark place
Where not even your own shadow exists
Darkness makes you take so much of risks
It is risks that make you grow rich quick
Makes you invalid and alienates the public

       The ugly bad thing about the money is
       It doesn't follow you everywhere you go
       Not just when it is time for the curtains
       So why make so much of the turgid money
       That drives you mad and divides so many
       Deserts you when you are in dire agony

But do make money in their company
Whose sweating and puffing brings it
Don't stock it in over valued property
Keep it in circulation it remains fresh
Retains its vigour to grow and empower
If you hold or splurge it you invite fear

       Money making is risking in the dark
       Firing from others' guns targets afar
       Gains are many but misses are large
       Money is neither a friend nor enemy
       Don't split it, got to handle it with care
       Lest it burns your soul 'n of your kin's

Try not to halve it, let it remain whole
If you do that it just gets sunk or stolen
It is octane fuel pass it on to everyone
Lest it engulfs you in conflagration
Its human, it has a large beaming face
You don't see it at all in the mock race

      Handle it with care for everyone's sake
      Hold it for a while pass it on to others
      To serve a deal buy sell 'n help mentors
      You will see it sets many faces on smile
      It doesn't stay with the one who rakes it
      Unless it is judiciously held spread wide

Let it flow freely lest it enslaves you
Bonded to money is worst than perfidy
In circulation it has a multiplier effect
Share it with others it just gets jet set
There is plenty 'n none need go empty
Provided its not locked out from many

Paradox

'Merchants have no country'
Business has no set policy
Profits no genuine entry
Sellers owe no guarantee

> Wise have no vision
> Visionary no sights
> Lies have no source
> Truth has no aliases

Men have no charity
Woman has no security
Law has no justice
Justice has no taker

> Justice is a purifier
> A summation of truth
> Compassion in essence
> Mother of all virtues

> But all that is possible only
> When honest people're around
> And govt. edicts are stable
> Alas! that's not the case at all

Thief a friend in need
Waste will make us think
Pollution will pull us off
From vandalism greed

Savants will save Gods
From busy senile priests
For us all to live in peace
Do deeds without caveat
Sure men won't be cheats

Me Meism

Its not capitalism communism nor even fashion
Its me-meism that has soured the thoughts of men
In the name of liberty equality build rich mansions
For the human rights Hqrs of self- serving morons

Else how could people masquerade as saviours
With nothing to give but dirt and dusky provision
Calling it social responsibility, trick the crestfallen
Those well fed, console the starving with sermons

Once body is cast to the bins soul does not linger
Lost to the heavens where only self-seekers gather
Fake is the civilization lecherous pushed by vanity
Like ugly dinosaurs feeds on the flesh of its progeny

Lucky dinosaurs had queer men to excavate them
Men will have none to extricate them from oblivion
Let this civilization move faster for end to come soon
Lest poor Earth is left with nothing to fall back on

Bogy Money

All the little money I earn from hard labour
In fields factories deadly mines shop floors
All that is contained in this tattered wallet
I hold it dear it's just not a simple container

Sweat and blood brain 'n brown wear 'n tear
Them all mingled to make it truly unique
Dear to one 'n all, filled with memories
Sweet and some sour common to us all

Take all money that's left in my wallet
And fill it with those point sharp pellets
So I could hit hard to cripple its snatcher
Because it holds all my molten memories

Hope hid in the corner despair in its folds
Strength and courage held fast in the hold
Contentment from life's struggles zipped
Nature created it to store flawed scripts

If money was all, there won't be disease
People would not die for want of relief
It is a facilitator not the end of business
Business sure dies if money is held high

Choice of ratios ensures no money supply
Just put people in the centre of business
See how well both money 'n business thrive
Business of business is to make people happy

Just do it that way and you will find its easy
There won't be takeovers crushing closures
Nor even the eerie cries of grisly bear-hugs
Nor any bull runs rouse fear of a frothy glut

Plaintive notes of money's vinegary life
Scare all virtues and swipe all the values
Its a bill of exchange shouldn't dictate life
Meant to secure the dreams of one and all

Janus faced many its charms deadly embrace
More you pair share, better it behaves
Enriches your lives and of others
Its a good friend relentless master though

Don't hold it tight would burn your conscience
Let it not scamper around, would dirty the place
With structures unworthy of pretence
So let it not ensnare you, just a servitor it is

Dinosaurian Dirge

Mom will I grow large 'n wide as you
Corpulent 'n unseemly from end to end
Foraging vast expanse of prime nature
Guzzling verdant flora and fauna alike
Moving from one zone we rendered arid
To another waiting for same kinda pride

Will I ever be able to go back to places
I loved as child full verdant lush green
Now vast stretches of forbidding ravines
Hollowed lands full of slush and slime
Rendered acrid by our gargantuan appetite
Only tree trunks bones of the creatures
We made disappear now alone survive

Mom we're forced to eat our own kinds
Why don't we repair to seas like whales
Heed grandpa's those last dying words:
***"It is better to grow two blades of grass
Where one grew 'n save our own habitat."***
We dinosaurs are rulers of vast domains
Rulers don't change habitat gait or style

We care not wretched planet goes to dogs
We'd jamborees bacchanalia sex what not
We have heritage of bones that we leave
We have nothing of worth left to save now
Son! jump on that ponderous trunk of tree
Wait for the lightning to strike to turn you
Into tiny seeds for new cycle to begin anew

Civilization Gone Spooky

Good god, our lust for life is waning
Limbs lengthen, confidence is weak
Prodded by ego 'n spurred by vanity
Wrecked on pallid shores of fantasy
Spirits caved into boundless self pity

In reality, our life is taking back tally
Unconcerned with roaring challenges
Unable to checkmate evil temptations
Even sustain hope in tender heartbeats
Only rouses illusions of world in haste

Men-folk are looking beyond horizon
For just a vestige of venison doe caviar
They are revelling mulishly in what is
Their perky cradle of lust and lush life
Create nothing but a ghastly caterwaul

Drunken night, that keeps mortals awake
With promise of dawn of a joyous life,
Lies prostrate uncared on stony floors
Of the freakish civilization gone spooky
Waiting for dawn to gather its remains

Art Mongers

Pull down the curtain
Let go off the lights
And the hall empty
There will be no play

I am a dansuse of skills
Exquisite charm high spirit
My repertoire is fabulous
Sublime mean splendid

Recklessly make me do
Same steps, time and again
Not caring for my ennui
My tremor anguish 'n pain

Choked within bruised outside
Steps are heavy, heart sunk
But your pleasure knows not
My agony my blisters many

As I writhe in scalding pain
You shout encore in half wit
I know it's futile any more
To argue with art-mongers

I am the play and its source
To me it's soulful exuberance
For you a *de rigueur* frivolity
Tittle tattle clumsy snobbery

Spark of Life

Good judgment resides in wisdom
Good wisdom in purity of mind
Purity of mind in faith in values
It comes from absence of greed
Loss of greed from hold on needs
Hold on needs promotes sharing
Sharing is celebration of nature

Nature nurtures will to survive
Mandates common destiny for all
Common destiny follows trust
Trust among men strengthens
Well springs of life in all of us
So foster trust the spark of life
Keep it glowing while you are alive

Plant the Tree of Life

Sow a habit to reap a character
Sow a character to reap a destiny
To reap a destiny plant tree of life
In your courtyard of perseverance

Fenced by lush vines of charity
Pride valour and ceaseless labour
Aligned with endearing verities of life
In the straight line of sight of virtues

Your tomorrow will thus lengthen
Into the ageless realm of recognition
Life's chores will be music divine
Provided you keep your vision aligned

With republican mandate of nature kind
Preserve perpetuate all that's around you
As nature's helmsman pedal softly her canoe
Making life for all scorn and squalor free

Great men of our age had no special talent
But passionately curious about their intent
Sure you too can shape your destiny right
By keeping coals of endeavour burning bright

Promise of Life

I read and I am overly lost
I write 'n am utterly confused
I think and I am shaken up
By sensation nothing lasts
Thought is stale a time past
All borrowed often bruised

>So I go to far away fields
>Random gardens valleys green
>Crannies harbouring lean men
>Singing 'n sweating in mirth
>Each drop bears promise of life
>Develops into plentiful sprouts

Lightening thunder cloud rain
Bring joys occasional despair
Self-same rivers burst banks
Quietly they move their hutments
Atop steep hills wait for dawn
They communicate with heavens
Don't need priests to say amen

Two Sides of Coin

I can't love or hate my body
Becoz I am so attached to it
Thinking of my body I make
Love and hate to alternate

It's the call of our conscience
That we should try to listen to
Those who do, know the essence
Hate and love aren't different

My body and me are one indeed
Them I can't twit or deride
Like two sides of a coin minted
In mass by feral blind mandate

Those who know value of coin
Bother not what side is down
Nor by the figure on it drawn
It's dumb number that counts

When the fake coin circulates
Then democracy runs smoothly
And when the numbers are large
It serves the crocodiles mostly

Man has sort of a prism in mind
Which traces rainbows at times
Myriad hues overlap in cosmos
Prism gone reality is a shadow

Rift Inside

Was it all evanescent that tounsled my mind
As if to chasten me to collect weary spirits
Or the result of chasing runaway thoughts
Else just a cry that impaled heart released

That was too deep indeed for it to surface come
Rarefied by unceasing qualms of enquiry
A meek voice slyly in contact with the soul
Quietly sounded the heart of the rift inside:

Mend entangled threads of the ebbing life
Bridge rising distances of mind and heart
Astride life's faint breath, benign soul calls
Think awhile, stitch doubts all will be fine

Temporal Coil

At the death of the pale day
When evening was burning
Amidst its waning grandeur
Clouds rolling dancing dolls
Turned into big golden balls

Placid horizon rising from afar
Had nothing was void of visage
None of nascent pulsating vistas
Yet in the twilight I could feel
My soul anchored in hope

A coy smile douched my heart
As darkness gathered silence
I heard It murmur distinctly
Soft notes redolent of mercy
Tears rolled down in ecstasy

As happiness cascaded within
I could see 'n feel It in solitude
Enveloped by halos around It
But now I seek only Its grace
Temporal coils makes me wait

Gifts of Muse

How much should you ask of life
Not much beyond simple seeking
A grain of mirth a a drop of nector
A moment full of human kindness

An hour of soulful love 'n respite
And unending dream of happiness
Withal, I shall carry all my days
Past aged night to back of beyond.

Yes you shall've them all no doubt
As you don't seek them in gestures
Of frigid customs and guiles of vices
But as rewards of plain good deeds

Chapter 8

Miscellaneous

Cut Tit Fit

It's a mystery why you cut that piece of cloth
Pin hem tuck stitch squirm fold and frill
Into shapes tiny winy that make little sense
Then call it a romance of crazy nude women

Provides no comfort nor covers blanched skin
More misshaped riotous hues the more wooed
Women ramp before wooden-headed parvenus
Its sex-biz not culture, it is worst than bird flu

Millions been drained 'n thousands famished
For a few to strut on squeaky wooden boards
Many innocent brave souls drenched in sweat
Herald the queen of bees mugged by dreams

But in the parlour of porn many hearts quailed
Lisping carols of arty waspy dank sophistry
Blase is this flip flop show endorsing vanity
In people who pollute taste 'n patent chicanery

Time the rampaging fire of fashion is doused
Lest hapless damsels are sold like stuffed goose
Carved shared among balding owl-eyed ogres
And short changed to promote sex and booze

Its a knotted mystery why people seek fashions
Have no valid theories nor set principles
Unkempt desires transgress boundaries of boredom
All that endures on the ramp is dark frustration

Yet like the wild bees in the dense forests
It attracts the young and old, bald and brutes
Vision confined to finely torn filmy clothing
Ill equipped frames, hard smelling perfumes

Stilettoes supporting lean bamboos put on clips
Romping on boards spurred by roitoues ambitions
If a skinny mermaid emerges, it's devoured by ogres
Foul mouthed connoisseurs impassioned voyeurs

Judges in bandaged minds, seated on mounds of graft
Discernment left at doors of greedy busybuddies
Crafters, sponsors stage managers of the show-biz
Have only one thing in common, to cheat each other

Never in history such buggered carnivals held
Had never had a respectable mass endorsement
Betray a sense of direction or purpose of life
Leave none happy nor ever make anyone contended

Those who lose, survive on crumbs, perished hopes
Fahion, sure ploughs through your freedom, sanity
Leaves behind charred ambitions, waisted lives
Life is precious for fashions to misguide

Well Wed Life

Don't eat and drink just to be merry
Be not in an uncalled for hurry burry
No body has so far won the rat race

Don't build castles to live in despair
Sell family silver for dividend unpaid
Only the thugs win in market place

It is a never ending circular maze
Why spend life in counting waves
Distant stars are our daily visitors

Marry in floods, abstain in droughts
Love in summer winter is distraught
Fly in hope never to settle in slopes

Learn to tie loose ends of life firmly
There's no treasure as well wed life
Have endearing love within the family

Earn scarce laurels in the earthy fest
Live happily unbothered for the next
Don't mess life it will move merrily

Our Bodies are Platforms

We don't eat food, we eat meaty decorations
We don't wear clothes, but tenny wenny fashions
We don't have a body, but cosmatic platforms
There is no beauty in life, it is all seductive designs

Creeds have prevented God from coming of age
Desires taking time to turn modest suave
Shifting focus on esoteric ill-written scripts
Making us wallow in our own putrid cesspit

Come sit by my side and see what is inside
Of you and me, if not just the breathing space
It has hardly any room for envy or hate
Yet we let them in as if doomsday is near

Have Sex to Heart's Content

Do have sex to your heart's content
Certainly not at all at body's intent
But if you don't you sure turn sterile
Those mad with sex can never seed

> Without seed there won't be plantation
> There won't be flowers without both
> Have sex to ensure that there is seed
> Plantation and fruit to enjoy in peace

Sex be like waxing waning of moon
Rising 'n setting of the glorious sun
The balmy touch of refreshing wind
Cooling vibrancy of the young spring

> Sex is to enliven and enhance life
> To close the chasm of restless mind
> And to put the zoom of spirit in bind
> Don't you put lissome sex in the grind

Have sex to heart's content in full moon
When world is fully wrapped in beams
Turn not silky night into maze of grey
Missing dawn's spread of pure ecstasy

Life is More than Prurient Fun

A dog is more than its empty bark
Woman is more than her sex mark
Man is more than his little cannon
Life's much more than a prurient fun

      Why linger on, sex be creamy though
      Beyond sex lies life's treasure trove
      Don't ever mix sex with sadist fun
      Hurts, deprives you of decent run

Tree has trunks branches and buds
Flowers 'n drops fruits once a year
Keeps the promise made to creator
Enjoys the full life for many years

      Puny little man among all creatures
      Doesn't flower and fruit in season
      Leaves a progeny unlike him or her
      Who is either slovenly or a sinner

Hope does rub-a-dub as if to say:
"Nature pre-empts to save our souls
So abandon pursuits ending in agony
Lest age hauls albatross of felony

Don't linger in dingy dark cells
Dazzling razzmatazz, wily sirens
Who burn your flesh, choke souls
Have no love for you your beans

Funs have bad habit of dying dry
Just when you are in high spirits.
Run away, follow nature's tidings
Time now to rewrite your scripts"

Facelift

You start fearing your face in the mirror
Don't ever know who's the real one either
The one who stands in front of the mirror
Or one in bathroom stuck pale with horror

       The passion to live life as in the mirror
       Makes you burn resources and basal skills
       Scaling heights of ego 'n boorish disdain
       Stuffed tiger looks clean than the live one

Reality is different from one in the mirror
Still all of us want image as in the mirror
Let's hope reality will return to the mirror
Clothed one is better than that in the other

       You are among your few admirers like you
       Their number is small crazy their moods
       Why indulge in such an errant nonsense
       You have a better view from a distance

Not for nothing they call me mirror
Free from all blemishes of greed 'n pride
There's nothings in me I can be proud of
I only reflect without equivocation 'n guiles

       Infact we are all just reflected glories
       Of men and things from ages gone by
       Got to mend the world, not a bucaneer be
       To own what wasn't yours or ever be

Let Me be Me

Why see nudity as a witty edit of art
Love at sight as a meaty pot-boiler
Sex as a spirited game sans referee
Lines goal posts or the whistle blower

       Come think why the two peeping holes
       Adorn the forehead of a flattened skull
       Rather pinned on the fleshy wavy bottoms
       To keep an eye on maverick pendulum

Scandals are a crop of the void minds
Brewed 'n fuelled by turgid big belly
By men living life of vacuous prudery
Have a secret a pouch of lust 'n thuggery

       In the love-lorn lust nothing is so sure
       Except companion deigns to withdraw
       Even before elliptic epilogue is written
       Whirligig of lust goes on nevertheless

Smothered by Sex

Why is it, sex has always to be as woman
Pirouetting before lecherous junky men
Smothered by lust in thought and action
Burnt bruised pilfer rubber from mattress
Try to live in pleasure but die in distress

      Wheels of love slip at the gate of sex biz
      Dovecote of desires is gloomy and vexed
      The puny men of short life, little wisdom
      Are swayed by sex bereft of judgement
      They have a short life sex in abundance

Passion and vanity rest over frothy waves
Leave no trace on sparkling mind space
Don't make lust a ticket to unhealthy sex
It draws you closer to hell far from heaven
Revelling in it you'll never get happiness

Sex Biz

There are images that are not genuine
There are women who have form only
There is sex on cards tape 'n warrens
Its no sex nor even trifle prurient fun

It's a flattened hole with surface creaky
It has neither a body shape nor breeze
Its broken piece of ugly exposed meat
To make it saleable leavened with yeast

Lacks charm warmth tingling sensation
A piggy bank wide slit to put money in
Entire business is to sell sex with a spin
Sum total is revolting cold frustration

Unbothered if you are male female or hip
Use cajolery coquetry to woo dim-wits
Unconcerned if cage is ready for the fun
Care not you've a gun or aid-made button

Sex is not a Quick Fix

Oh woman oh woman
Don't dare your wares
They aren't sane you see
Who cares maiden or slut
Just have no discernment.

Don't go sexy-waxy places
Breasts bursting skin visible
Bums flitting body supple
A free joyride for junkies
Bereft of any goal in life.

Sex is not a quick fix
Hits misses and chances
Sex isn't mere eroticism
Wild orgy and vandalism
Nor a casual indulgence

Its smile on lovely face
Hands in control hair set
Feet firm and walk easy
Live within bonds of sex
Going beyond you'd mess